THE RETURN OF
LAFAYETTE

BY MARIAN KLAMKIN

The Return of Lafayette

American Patriotic and Political China

White House China

MARIAN KLAMKIN

THE RETURN OF
LAFAYETTE

1824 - 1825

CHARLES SCRIBNER'S SONS
NEW YORK

Library of Congress Cataloging in Publication Data

Klamkin, Marian.
     The return of Lafayette, 1824–1825.

     Bibliography: p.
     1. Lafayette, Marie Joseph Paul Yves Roch Gilbert
du Motier, Marquis de, 1757–1834. I. Title.
E207. L2K55   973.5′4′0924 [B]   74–8956
ISBN 0–684–13887–5

1 3 5 7 9 11 13 15 17 19 C/MD 20 18 16 14 12 10 8 6 4 2

Printed in the United States of America

TO JOAN AND BRAD

CONTENTS

CONTENTS

THE RETURN OF
LAFAYETTE

1

INTRODUCTION

No event in the early nineteenth-century history of the United States was the cause of such great excitement, unification, and celebration among its citizens as the return to these shores, after an absence of over forty years, of the Revolutionary War hero, General Marie-Joseph-Paul-Yves-Roch-Gilbert Motier Lafayette. The visit took place in the year 1824–25 and American patriotism reached an unprecedented peak in a time of peace. The year-long visit of the nation's guest served two important purposes: first, it gave the country an opportunity to show its gratitude to the only surviving major-general of the War for Independence; second, it restored to an aging Lafayette his dignity, pride, and fortune, all of which had been sorely depleted through his long years spent in fighting for individual freedom in his own country.

If history can be learned through the objects and documents that survive it, the souvenirs that were made for the visit of Lafayette and other related ephemera tell us the story of one year in American history. From a study of Lafayette-related material of 1824–25 we learn about the state of American industrial art and the great progress that had been made in the half-century that had passed since the Revolution. Documents and letters that still exist describe the unprecedented hospitality of a grateful nation and American patriotism worked up to a fever pitch.

Lafayette was fêted in every town through which he passed and menus and descriptions of these entertainments make vivid pictures of social life in America in that one special year. Military

1. Portrait of Lafayette as he looked in 1824. *From an old engraving taken from an original painting by Chappel*

historians, through a study of the documents from 1824–25 that still exist, can get a clearer picture of how the various state militia were organized and the speed with which they could muster when called upon for special events. Every town, no matter how small, was able to present a respectable welcoming parade, frequently upon very short notice.

If the visit was advantageous to Lafayette, it served to aid many American infant industries. Printers, glassblowers, and other craftsmen vied with one another to be the first to produce souvenir products that bore Lafayette's image and slogans such as "Welcome, Lafayette, the Nation's Guest," "A Nation's Gratitude," "Republicans Are Not Always Ungrateful," and other similar tributes. Ribbons were produced with Lafayette's image, often alongside that of George Washington, which were worn by welcoming committees and military and fraternal organizations. Songwriters and poets had a new subject about which to write and they did so with amazing speed. Plays were written specifically for Lafayette's frequent visits to all the theaters in the country that were then open. Many of these plays related events in Lafayette's life, a favorite subject being Lafayette's imprisonment at Olmütz, in Austria, during the French Revolution.

Wherever Lafayette went during his amazing tour of America there were some souvenirs made locally by enterprising businessmen and craftsmen, who also put effort and much thought into making unique and historically significant gifts for Lafayette. Some of these gifts were recorded at the time by Lafayette's secretary, Auguste Levasseur, who, along with Lafayette's only son, George Washington Lafayette, accompanied the hero on his tour of the United States. Along with his secretarial duties, Levasseur was given the task of keeping a complete journal of the visit. At times this must have been difficult and the secretary was unable to keep his dates straight, although his descriptions of events are the only full eyewitness report we have of the entire year of arduous traveling. Levasseur's account of the trip was published in France in

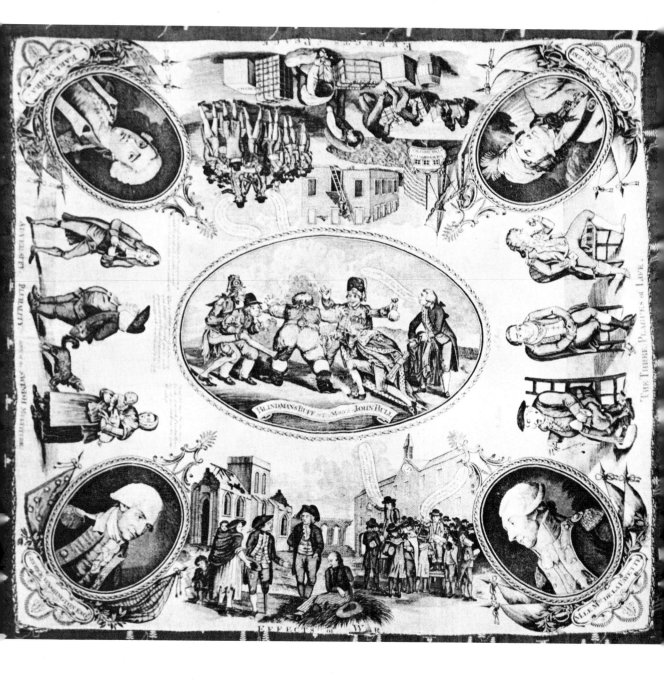

3. Papier mâché snuff-box inset with silver medallion showing
profiles of Washington and Lafayette. Late eighteenth century.
De Witt Collection, University of Hartford

2. *Opposite.* Rare political bandana showing
Lafayette as a younger man and a hero of
the Revolution. *Circa* 1795. *Collection of
E. Norman Flayderman*

1828 and two American translations were published in America in 1829. His two-volume work is now a collector's item along with many other publications that describe with even less accuracy Lafayette's visit.

It is interesting, and perhaps somewhat ironic, that the most abundant and probably the most profitable of souvenirs made for Lafayette's visit to America was the pottery manufactured and printed in England and shipped to a nation eager to own something that would remind citizens in each town of the day Lafayette's coach appeared and the great and memorable celebrations that took place. The British potters printed all possible welcoming slogans on their plates and quickly adapted to the printing process any recent portrait of Lafayette that was available. In addition, the potters produced plates and other dinnerware with patriotic scenes of all of the historic and natural sites visited by Lafayette.

The American glass industry was fairly well established by 1824 and was primarily involved in making an adequate supply of bottles and flasks. Molds were designed with Lafayette's image incised in them only days after Lafayette's foot touched American soil. These whiskey flasks were extremely popular in a year of intense patriotism and celebration. Thousands of toasts were drunk to Lafayette at dinners that he attended and at many that he did not. To judge from the amount of Lafayette flasks that were produced, however, it is probable that at almost every American inn and tavern in 1824–25 that Lafayette did not visit, he was at least there in spirits. Lafayette flasks are now premium items for collectors of early bottles and glassware.

Were it not for Levasseur's travelogue, souvenir books printed to commemorate Lafayette's visit to certain cities, press reports, and some private correspondence from that year it would be difficult to imagine the scope and importance to the American people of Lafayette's unique tour. Although the souvenirs and relics of that year are scattered among private collectors, museums, and historical societies of the twenty-four states that made up the United

States in 1824, the recording of some of these objects can give the student of American history a vivid picture of a nation, which although widely scattered geographically, unified to entertain and applaud a man who meant so much to its early history. A record of the itinerary itself also should give the historian-collector some idea of where to look for Lafayette-related material.

2

THE INVITATION, THE VOYAGE, AND LAFAYETTE'S ARRIVAL IN NEW YORK

A visit to this country by Lafayette was not an event that was decided hastily or without important motivation. By 1824 it was evident to the hero's many friends that his efforts in behalf of establishing a government in France based on the American constitution had been in vain. He had lost his power in France and was out of favor with the government. However, he had a stubborn nature and had no compunctions about confronting the French government. Along with his influence, he also had lost his inherited fortune. Some of his funds had been spent freely in the cause of American freedom and the rest was confiscated during the French Revolution. His family was living at his country seat, La Grange, at the time Lafayette received his invitation to America, but it was a problem making ends meet and it had long been understood that a visit to American shores would require a gift of some sort of restoration of the Lafayette family fortunes. It seemed a good time for Lafayette to leave France. His decision to do so brought grateful sighs of relief from his many friends on both sides of the ocean who feared for his life. When an invitation was voted by the American Congress and extended in a letter by President James Monroe, Lafayette was, according to Auguste Levasseur, "free from engagements." Monroe wrote:

4. Lafayette family crest with motto "Why not?"
Photograph courtesy State Street Bank and
Trust Company, Boston

Washington City
February 24, 1824

My Dear General,

I wrote you a letter about fifteen days since, by Mr. Brown, in which I expressed the wish to send to any port in France you should point out, a frigate to convey you hither, in case you should be able to visit the United States. Since then, Congress passed a resolution on this subject, in which the sincere attachment of the whole nation to you is expressed, whose ardent desire is once again to see you amongst them. The period at which you may yield to this invitation is left entirely at your option, but believe me, whatever your decision, it will be sufficient that you should have the goodness to inform me of it, and immediate orders will be given for a government vessel to proceed to any port you will indicate, and convey you thence to the adopted country of your early youth, which has always preserved the most grateful recollection of your important services. I send you herewith the resolution of congress and add thereto the assurance of my high consideration and of my sentiments of affection.

Besides his need for restoring some of the Lafayette family fortunes by whatever means the American people decided was appropriate, Lafayette was anxious to see for himself some positive results of his lifelong struggle for democracy. He was sixty-six, an age when such a visit, long discussed in his family, could not be put off. Before he could leave France, however, he had to settle some of his debts and this caused a delay in his departure. The American minister to France loaned him money for this purpose and Lafayette, proudly refusing the offer of an American ship to be paid for by the government, instead booked passage on the *Cadmus,* an American frigate, for himself, his son, his secretary, and his valet. It was understood from the outset of the voyage that Lafayette was to be the guest of the entire nation rather than be entertained exclusively by certain select groups.

An article in the *National Journal* of Washington, D. C., on August 5, 1824, set the climate for the visit and related to Americans something of Lafayette's financial problems. The article was reprinted in newspapers throughout the country:

General Lafayette It is not improbable that the arrangements, of the completion of which Gen. Lafayette speaks as being necessary before his departure from France for this country were arrangements of a pecuniary kind. It is well known that the General is not rich. Probably of the vast estates of which he was proprietor in his own right and that of his wife, at the commencement of our revolution, nothing remains except the estate called Le [sic] Grange where he and his family reside.

It is understood that he will be at no expense. He ought to be at no expense anywhere. It is hoped that he will not be permitted to expend one cent in the United States,—the people have proclaimed him to be their guest; Let him be treated therefore, as such. Whenever he leaves a city, a gentleman should be appointed to attend him, and to guard him from every expense until he arrives at some other city, where he will receive a similar attention.

The reporter's advice was taken literally by the entire nation. All tolls were free to Lafayette's party, coaches, and horses; boats were provided when necessary, as well; and not one gentleman, but many, accompanied Lafayette from one town to the next. The visit was lucrative to many citizens, however. Innkeepers and tavernkeepers served and bedded the hoards of people who traveled long distances for a glimpse of the hero. Hundreds of new flags and banners were made. The aforementioned printers hastily found portraits of Lafayette to copy and made labels that were pasted to snuff boxes and sold as souvenirs.

By the time the four French travelers had left Paris for Havre, where they boarded the *Cadmus* on July 11, elaborate plans were already in motion to receive the hero with an appropriate welcome. The ship sailed on the thirteenth under the command of Captain Allyn, and except for a squall on the second day out and a delay when the ship was becalmed on the first of August, the voyage was uneventful. Land was sighted on August 14 and the following morning at daybreak a pilot came on board and Levasseur noted, "We could easily distinguish the fresh verdure which adorns Staten Island, the charming white dwellings which enlivened it, and the movement of its inhabitants, which the expectation of some great event had caused all haste to run down to the shore."

The "great event" was, of course, the long-awaited arrival of Lafayette, and as cannons thundered a welcome from the direction of Fort Lafayette in Brooklyn the ship was surrounded by many kinds of boats filled with shouting crowds. This scene was painted and printed many times during the year.

A steamboat bearing the Vice-President of the United States approached the *Cadmus* and Daniel Tompkins informed Lafayette that because the ship had arrived on Sunday the people of New York were unwilling, even for this great event, to break the Sabbath. It would be necessary, therefore, for Lafayette's entry into the city to be postponed until the following day. Moreover, said Tompkins, the citizens had not been certain exactly what day the *Cadmus* would arrive and further preparations would be necessary for a proper welcome. Lafayette and his fellow travelers spent the night at the Staten Island home of the Vice-President.

The following afternoon, at one o'clock, Lafayette and his party, which by now included the municipal representatives, two hundred principal citizens of New York, the commanding generals of the Army and their counterparts of the Navy, and many of Lafayette's old comrades-in-arms, boarded the steamboat *Chancellor Livingston,* which Levasseur described as a "floating palace." Other ships and boats joined the fleet, including the *Cadmus,* pulled by two tugs. Pennants and flags were flown from every mast and rope and the shore was crowded with an estimated two hundred thousand people. Lafayette landed at the Battery at two o'-clock.

An escort of the Lafayette Guards was drawn into a line to receive the General and the soldiers all wore badges printed with Lafayette's portrait and the words "Welcome Lafayette." A procession was formed and Lafayette was escorted into a waiting carriage drawn by four white horses that would carry him to City Hall. The streets were lined with flags and bunting draped the buildings.

Flowers and wreaths were thrown into Lafayette's carriage as it passed and it was obvious that the citizens of New York had spent the Sabbath hard at work rather than in prayer and contemplation. The question of what should or should not be done on Sunday in relation to Lafayette's visit, especially in the more puritan towns of New England, would come up more than once in the year ahead. When the General, in a hurry to fulfill obligations in a distant town or city, ignored the Sunday restrictions on travel, he counted on his popularity and the people's affection toward him to excuse his transgressions. Disgruntled citizens wrote irate letters to their local newspapers, and this was the cause of the only disapproval Lafayette was to receive.

A major factor in the enormous success of Lafayette's tour of America was his ability to speak, read, and write English with some fluency. His son also had had an education in English and had spent several years in the United States during the period when his father, and later his mother and sisters, were prisoners in the Austrian prison at Olmütz. Levasseur evidently spoke little English and seemed to be thrilled every time he met French-Americans with whom he could converse easily.

Welcoming speeches and a response by Lafayette were given in City Hall and he reviewed the militia as it filed off after the ceremony. For the following two hours the General received the public in the great salon of the municipal building. Levasseur recorded his impression of the public reception. It was to be repeated in every city and many towns and villages of the United States in the next twelve months:

Mothers surrounded him, presenting their children and asking his blessing, which having obtained, they embraced their offspring with renewed tenderness; feeble old men appeared to become reanimated in talking to him of the numerous battles in which they had been engaged with him for the sake of liberty. Men of colour reminded him with tenderness of his philanthropical efforts at various periods, to replace them in rank, which horrid prejudices still deny them in some countries; young men with hard

5. Papier mâché snuff box showing "Landing of Gen. La Fayette at Castle Garden, New York, 16th August 1824" was souvenir item of the event. Around rim, "Entered According to Act of Congress the 27th Day of October 1824 by Samuel Maverick of the State of New York." Maverick copperplate print was pirated by Rollinson and others. *Collection of William H. Guthman*

6. Papier mâché snuff box with engraving of scene at Castle Garden when Lafayette landed. "Welcome Lafayette in the United States of America." *Collection of William H. Guthman*

7. Blue-and-white printed plate, "Landing of Gen. La Fayette at Castle Garden New York 16th August 1824." Design was pirated from Maverick engraving used for snuff boxes. Made by James and Ralph Clews, Staffordshire, England, in 1825. *Mattatuck Museum*

8. "Cadmus at anchor." Plate printed in dark blue and made by Enoch Wood & Sons. *Circa* 1825. *Mattatuck Museum*

and blackened hands announced their laborious occupations, stopped before him and said with energy, "We also belong to the ten millions who are indebted to you for liberty and happiness!" Many others wished to speak to him, but were prevented by their tears; those who could not approach him, endeavoured to compensate for it by addressing George Lafayette, whom they pressed in their arms, while talking to him of their admiration for his father.

A huge state banquet was held at City Hall at five o'clock, which was then the regular dinner hour, and at six o'clock the balloon *American Eclipse* ascended over the New York skyline in honor of Lafayette's first day in America.

The celebrations in New York were to establish a pattern for the rest of the country in the reception of Lafayette. His good friend Thomas Jefferson was to write of him, "Lafayette had a canine appetite for popularity and fame." This undoubtedly was true, for on a schedule most of the year that would have exhausted the most seasoned politician, the sixty-seven-year-old Frenchman seemed to thrive. He never appeared to tire of hearing his name shouted or his virtues and glorious deeds recounted. He attended many theatrical performances recounting his deeds and listened to hundreds of poems and songs written in his honor. Each time he was so moved that reporters described his tears.

Lafayette's tour of America is unique in history. There was impartiality everywhere when it came to celebrating the hero's arrival. The country was truly Lafayette-crazed and the story of that one unanimously happy and unified year in American history is unique.

3

RECEPTION BY THE
PEOPLE OF NEW YORK

The scene at New York's City Hall was repeated for two-hour sessions for the next four days. Lafayette submitted gladly to the embraces, tears, and hysterics of the great crowds of people who came to meet, touch, and be near the hero. During this period also, deputations from other cities and towns and representatives of state governments came to extend their welcome and to elicit from Lafayette promises that he would visit their areas. The remainder of this first short stay in New York was spent in being guest of honor at all the learned societies of the city. The New-York Historical Society made Lafayette and his son honorary members and as an extra honor seated the guest in a chair that had been owned by Gouverneur Morris and before that to the unfortunate Louis XVI. Members of the bar and the French residents of New York also paid homage to the distinguished visitor. Banquets, lengthy addresses, and numerous toasts accompanied all of these occasions.

One group that welcomed Lafayette in almost every city and town on his journey was the Society of the Cincinnati. Lafayette had joined this elite group of American army officers in France although he had had some qualms about it being truly democratic. When George Washington had written him about the formation of the group in this country in 1784 Lafayette wrote back to say that most Americans in Paris opposed it. He objected to the condition of hereditary rights, which he said seemed to him to endanger the "true principles of democracy." He was willing to do whatever his hero and mentor, Washington, thought best and upon his advice became a member.

The society did not become a threat. By 1824 many of the original members had died and the next generation had little in common with the old men who met to talk about their army days. Lafayette's visit helped revive the society and chapters in every town organized Lafayette receptions and played an important role in the year's success.

Major events in Lafayette's first week in New York, besides those already mentioned, were a gala performance of *Twelfth Night* on Tuesday, August 17, and a celebration at the Brooklyn Navy Yard on the eighteenth. While there he was given a tour of the new steam-frigate *Washington* and lunch was served to him aboard the vessel. That evening, after the Historical Society meeting, he attended a state dinner at City Hotel.

Lafayette's secretary had mixed impressions of the city on his first visit. He described the view of the city from Brooklyn as "picturesque" and "commanding." "Excepting the City Hall," wrote Levasseur, "there is not a single public edifice worthy of the attention of an artist." He felt that Brooklyn "should be considered a suburb of New York" and was puzzled that the city of New York was not the seat of government of the state. It was explained to him that the capital was planned to be located geographically in the center of the state.

While attending a banquet in Lafayette's honor a dinner companion explained something of the economics, politics, and attidues of his fellow citizens. Levasseur shared his employer's views on equality and democracy for every citizen and felt strongly enough about the treatment of blacks in New York in 1824 to repeat his companion's frail explanation of it. He was told, "Every white man, having attained the age of twenty-one years, resided six months in the state, and paid some tax during the electoral year, has the right of voting. Every man of colour, twenty-one years old, having been three years a citizen, a holder of property, and paying

9. Ribbon with portrait of Lafayette and "A Nation's Gratitude." *De Witt Collection, University of Hartford*

10. *Right.* Lafayette ribbon, "Our Nation's Guest." "Engraved and Sold by J. Yeager first door below the Post Office." *De Witt Collection, University of Hartford*

a tax of two hundred and fifty dollars, has also the right of suffrage." Levasseur's elderly companion went on to say, "This distinction of colour may surprise you, I shall not attempt to justify it, but shall content myself with requesting you, before you condemn it, to wait until you shall have passed through the different parts of our union before you form your judgement of the relative conditions of the two races."

Although it can be assumed that Levasseur politely withheld his opinions concerning the American treatment of "men of colour" that evening, he later commented many times in his account of the trip about the condition of blacks in the twenty-four states. Both he and Lafayette argued for equal rights, especially when they were guests of the founders of democracy, Thomas Jefferson and James Madison, both of whom ran their estates with slave labor.

On the nineteenth of August Lafayette received delegations from Baltimore, Philadelphia, and other cities, and arrangements for visits were set in motion. The French Society reception was held that afternoon and was followed by a parade of the New York Fire Department. Entertainments in New York could have continued for many more days, but Lafayette had made a promise to visit Boston as soon as possible upon his arrival. When he had received an invitation from Mayor Quincy shortly after the letter from Monroe had arrived he had answered as follows:

Sir—Amidst the new and high marks of benevolence the people of the United States and their representatives have lately deigned to confer upon me, I am proud and happy to recognize those particular sentiments of the citizens of Boston, which have blessed and delighted the first years of my public career, and the grateful sense of which has ever since been to me a most valued reward and support. —Whatever port I first attain, I shall with the same eagerness hasten to Boston, and present its beloved, revered inhabitants, as I have the honor to offer it to the City Council and to you, Sir, with the homage of my Affectionate gratitude and devoted respect.

In answer to another invitation to visit Boston, this one from former Senator James Lloyd, Jr., who had asked Lafayette to be a guest in his house, he wrote, "Whatever be the part of the United States, where I will find myself on my attaining the beloved shore, I shall not lose time in my eagerness to revisit the city of Boston, and answer the flattering invitation I have lately received."

The citizens of Boston were disappointed that the *Cadmus* had landed in New York and when the New York Committee urged Lafayette to lengthen his stay in that city he answered, "I cannot, for I wish to be in Boston that I may visit Cambridge on Commencement Day, where I shall meet many of my old friends. You know my attachment to you all, I am heartily glad to see, but I must make a visit immediately to Boston, and will return again."

4

NEW HAVEN AND PROVIDENCE

By the time Lafayette left for Boston, at dawn on Friday, August 20, 1824, plans were already being made for his reception in the towns through which he would pass. Correspondence was busily exchanged between officials of city and state governments and between committees of reception and the militia. The few pieces of correspondence that still exist attest to the fact that extraordinary arrangements could be made in an era of relatively slow communications within a very short time. Although New York had been the first city to pay its respects to the returning hero, smaller towns such as New Haven and Providence were not to be outdone. Lafayette's trip to Boston was considerably delayed, since every village along his route had made plans to receive him. The trip took five days and five nights and Levasseur wrote, "Our march was very slow, as we could not pass a hamlet without being detained some moments by collections of people from more than twenty miles around."

Lafayette departed New York with an assembly of escort that accompanied him through Harlem and West Farms as far as New Rochelle, where the first stop was made so that Lafayette could meet with some old soldiers who had been too feeble to make the trip to New York for his arrival. An escort of cavalry met the procession at Sawpits and continued to Putnam's Mountain, where a great triumphal arch had been erected in celebration of Lafayette's visit and in commemoration of General Putnam, the Revolutionary War hero. Relays of horses and drivers had already been arranged for the entire route.

The route chosen to Boston was over the Old Lower Post Road through Greenwich, Stamford, Norwalk, Saugatuck, and Fairfield, Connecticut. Even though there were stops in most towns along the way some citizens seemed to have had their problems in catching a glimpse of the nation's guest. A reporter on the *Commercial Advertiser,* of New York, complained, "The General traveled so fast, that many persons could not get a sight of him in their own towns; but many of them, on learning that he was to stop at the next, set off in haste to overtake him; and in some instances where they missed him in the next town, still pressed forward on foot."

The group traveled until near midnight and set out again at five in the morning. Fires were lighted from place to place from the tops of hills where groups of people had gathered in the hope of seeing the General's carriage as it passed. People in Fairfield were disappointed, since Lafayette's announced plans to arrive early in the evening had to be changed, and by the time he arrived at the Washington Hotel, many of them had gone home, for the workday started at dawn in the early nineteenth century. Inasmuch as Lafayette continued his journey at seven the next morning there was little time for revelry in the town of Bridgeport.

The hurried trip through Connecticut was described by the *Commercial Advertiser* reporter:

It is impossible to travel through the towns of Connecticut and not feel a part of the enthusiasm which pervaded all classes. Even the poor lads who drove the carriages entered fully into the common feeling, and seemed proud of their honours. They wore silk ribbons fastened to the buttonholes of their waistcoats, by way of distinction; and while waiting to receive their illustrious passenger, usually became persons of no considerable interest and attention with the hundreds who stood around. "Behave pretty now, Charley," said the driver of LaFayette's coach, to one of his horses, "behave pretty, Charley—you are going to carry the greatest man in the world."

On August 21 Lafayette's entourage passed through Stratford and into New Haven, which was splendidly decorated for the occasion. He was received by city authorities and the faculty of Yale College, and was a guest of the Common Council at a meal served at eleven o'clock. He received the students of Yale and at noon he reviewed the troops on the New Haven Green. Following this he was given a tour of Yale, which then had a faculty of four professors and six tutors and a student body of four hundred.

There are conflicting reports about where Lafayette spent Saturday night. His secretary vividly recalled that Lafayette was still in New Haven on Sunday morning and not wishing to act contrary to the habits of the people attended two church services where all citizens, regardless of sect, crowded into the churches on the Green so that they might tell their grandchildren they had been to church with Lafayette. According to reports in *The Boston Evening Gazette* (August 28, 1824) Lafayette spent the night in Saybrook and left on Sunday morning to breakfast at the home of Richard M'Curdy, Esq., at Lyme. In any case he arrived at Norwich at six o'clock, where he attended a reception, and spent Sunday night in Plainfield.

The previous week the city of Providence, Rhode Island, had held a town meeting and passed a resolution that "the citizens of Providence rejoice at the intelligence of the safe arrival of General Lafayette in the United States." A committee was formed and arrangements made for expenses to be drawn from the town treasury. Because Lafayette was in the unique position of being an invited guest of the people expenses were paid by each town where a reception was held. Two prominent Providence citizens were sent to Connecticut to invite Lafayette to the reception, for which elaborate plans were already being made, and although he could spend little time in that city the planned program was carried out in full.

When Lafayette arrived in Providence at noon on Monday, August 23, a huge procession had already been formed. It consisted of citizens mounted and on foot, officers and students of Brown University, a band of music, companies of military, the committee of arrangements on horseback, members of the town council in carriages, the Society of the Cincinnati, officers of the United States Government, Army and Navy, and many other dignitaries in carriages. Lafayette was given an open carriage drawn by four gray horses and flanked on either side by marshals. As reported in the Providence *Gazette* every horse and vehicle in the town appeared to be in requisition, and the windows on the streets through which the procession was to pass were thronged with women, waiting to greet the "Nation's Guest." Speeches were made at the town line, where the procession gathered, and as it traveled slowly along the route up Westminster Street to the State House Lafayette shook all the hands he could reach. The women waved white handkerchiefs from the windows where they had been stationed. "Many females," reported the *Gazette,* "in the excess of their feelings, suspended this token of welcome, to gaze more intently at the object whom they appeared alone to see in the whole procession, and many a fine eye was wet with the gush of a tear, which the rush of so many sublime and sympathetick emotions sent warm from the heart."

Lafayette's reception as he arrived at the State House was described by the same reporter:

On arriving in front of the State House, the General alighted, and was received in a peculiarly interesting manner. The poplar avenue, leading to the building was lined on each side with nearly two hundred misses arrayed in white, protected by a file of soldiers on each side, and holding in their hands bunches of flowers, which (as the General proceeded up the avenue, (supported by the Governor's Aids) they strewed in his path, at the same time waving their white handkerchiefs. The General was afterwards pleased to express the peculiar and high satisfaction he took in this simple and touching arrangement.

On reaching the landing of the stairs, the General turned toward the multitude, and at the same moment, the veteran Captain Stephen Olney (who served under the General repeatedly, and was the first to force the enemy's works at Yorktown, in which he was seconded, at another point,

11. Almost as soon as the Cadmus landed plans were made to entertain Lafayette in cities he would visit. Letter from mayor of New Haven to governor of Connecticut:

City of New Haven Aug 17, 1824

Sir

   I have only time to say before the mail closes that Genl La Fayette with his son arrived at New York on Sunday morning.

   Should he visit New Haven, we shall hope for the honor of your Excellency's company for the occasion.

Connecticut Historical Society

12. Letter from Mayor Hoadly of New Haven to Governor Wolcott, dated August 19, 1824:

Dr. Sir

General La Fayette will leave New York tomorrow morning at 7 o'clock and expects to arrive here tomorrow morning on his way to Boston. He will breakfast here on Saturday morning and travel to New London in the course of the day, having engaged to be at Boston next Tuesday morning.

I am requested to give you this information by the Committee of Arrangements, and to add that it will give the citizens of New Haven great pleasure to see you here on this occasion.

Connecticut Historical Society

CITY OF NEW-HAVEN, }
Friday, Aug. 20th. }

THE MAYOR and ALDERMEN present their compliments to *Govenor Wolcot*
and request the pleasure of his company at a Public
Breakfast, given by the City, at 8 o'clock to-morrow,
at Morse's Hotel, to the General LA FAYETTE.

By order.

GEO: HOADLY,
Mayor.

13. Formal invitation from city of New Haven to Governor Wolcott
to attend Lafayette breakfast on August 20. *Connecticut Historical Society*

WELCOME LAFAYETTE.

L oud does t he clarions' shrill and lofty strain,
A midst a people's joyful shouts, proclaim,
F am'd Chief, thy hearty welcome on our shore,
A nnoy'd by stern alarms of war no more.
Y et should some foe, invade the rights we won,
E nlink'd would be all patriot hearts in one—
T o guard them still. their faith be plac'd in one.
T hat to the World did make this just decree,
E ach man is Equal, and by Nature, Free.

" Hail to the Chief."

14. Acrostic, printed in *Independent Inquirer and Commercial
Advertiser* in Providence, Rhode Island, on Thursday morning,
August 26, 1824. To be sung to tune of "Hail to the Chief."

Collection of William H. Guthman

General,

I congratulate you on your arrival in the United States and I bid you welcome to the good old republican State of Connecticut, where you will find none but sincere Friends, who feel grateful for your distinguished services in favour of their Country and admirers of your Eminent Exertions in support of their principles both here & in Europe.

Minutes of address to Genl. La Fayette at New Haven August. 1824

15. Minutes of address by New Haven's mayor to General Lafayette:

General,
    I congratulate you on your arrival in the United States and I bid you welcome to the good old republican State of Connecticut, where you will find none but sincere Friends, who feel grateful for your distinguished services in favour of their country and admirers of your eminent exertions in support of their principles, both here and in Europe.

Connecticut Historical Society

almost simultaneously by Lafayette) approached the General, who instantly recognized his old companion in arms, and embraced and kissed him in the most earnest and affectionate manner. A thrill went through the whole assembly, and scarcely a dry eye was to be found among the spectators, while the shouts of the multitude, at first suppressed, and then, uttered in a manner tempered by the scene, evinced the deep feeling and proud associations it had excited.

There was another touching moment when an eighty-five-year-old veteran, William Russell, was led up to be presented to Lafayette. As Lafayette toured the country every veteran who was even partially ambulatory had an opportunity to be received by his old General and the tears shed by many were described by reporters everywhere.

After speeches, a dinner reception, and a review of the Rhode Island militia, Lafayette, escorted by the Society of the Cincinnati and other notables, traveled through Walpole and Dedham. Houses and gardens along the route were illuminated and crowds gathered at every crossroad. Lafayette arrived at one o'clock Tuesday morning at the home of Governor Eustis in Roxbury, Massachusetts.

5

THE BOSTON RECEPTION

"Two hours sleep," recalled Levasseur, "made us forget the fatigues of the day and rendered us fit for entering Boston in the morning." Awakened at daybreak to the sound of martial music played by a band of light infantry, Lafayette, his party, and the Governor prepared to be escorted to Roxbury at ten o'clock in the morning on the twenty-fourth and were met by the Mayor of Boston at the city line. During the welcoming ceremony free punch was handed out to the citizenry. Lafayette was then escorted to an open barouche drawn by four white horses and the slow procession into Boston began. Waiting at the Boston State House was a huge crowd led by a double row of girls and boys from the public schools. All were wearing Lafayette badges and one of the youngest girls set a wreath of evergreens upon Lafayette's head. When the General entered the door of the building a volley of guns was fired and the American flag was raised on the dome. Inside waited representatives of all the learned and fraternal societies of Boston and two hours of welcoming speeches commenced.

Apartments had been arranged for Lafayette in a residence on the corner of Beacon and Park streets. The rooms were described by Levasseur as being "richly furnished" and horses and carriages were placed at the travelers' disposal throughout their stay in Boston. The evening's entertainment included a huge banquet at the Boston Exchange Coffee House. The menu for that dinner, illustrated here, is typical of the huge meals served to Lafayette and his

Public Dinner,

GIVEN AT THE

EXCHANGE COFFEE HOUSE.

CONGRESS SQUARE.........BOSTON.,.......TUESDAY, AUGUST 24.

IN HONOR OF GENERAL LA FAYETTE.

BILL OF FARE.

FIRST COURSE.	SECOND COURSE.
Fish.	Roast Goose.
Halibut,	Ditto Chickens,
Cod's head and shoulders,	Ducks with Green Peas.
Tataug,	Woodcocks,
Hams Boiled,	Pidgeons,
Tongues, boiled.	Snipes.
Mutton boiled,	Le Maccarone,
Chickens boiled,	Lobster Friccassee,
Corned Beef boiled.	Les Omlettes, confitures,
Roast Lamb,	Les Beignets, des Pommes,
Ditto Pigs,	Calves' Feet.
Ditto Ducks,	———
Roast Goose, Mongrel,	Orange Cream
Roast Beef,	Puddings,
Ditto Chickens,	Calves' Feet Jelly.
Ditto Veal,	Sweetbreads Braiye.
Cotelette de Mouton Italienne	La Blancmange,
De Veau Fricondeau Glaze.	Pastry,
La Petite Pote Voloille.	Custards.
La vol au vent de Bouf.	
Pigeons En Compote.	———
Du Bouf de Marinade.	Ice Creams,
Du Veau Ragout.	Desert, &c.
Le Poulards Fricassee.	———
Harricot de Mouton.	JAMES HAMILTON.

W. W. Clapp, Print.

16. Menu for banquet given in honor of Lafayette at Exchange Coffee House, in Boston, on Tuesday, August 24, 1824.
Courtesy American Antiquarian Society

party almost every night of their year in America. The dinner concluded with a multitude of toasts.

The day had been one of great excitement for Boston's citizens and the daughter of the mayor, Miss E. S. Quincy, attended many of the entertainments given in Lafayette's honor and described the events in her diary:

At this time our family excepting my father and brothers were residing at Quincy but the arrival of La Fayette summoned us from the retirement of the country. On the evening of Sunday August 22nd I drove into Boston with one of my sisters. On arriving at our house in Hamilton Place, we found the drawing rooms crowded with the Committee of arrangements for the reception of La Fayette, all talking most vehemently, voice rising above voice, and the Mayor's above them all. We retreated to the dining-room, but there in addition to the tumult upstairs, was my brother, reciting a Latin oration he was preparing to speak at Commencement the next day.

—Early in the morning of Tuesday the 24th I went home for a short time to see my mother. Our family I found already in motion having in truth enjoyed but little rest, their repose during the night having been interrupted by three expresses. The first came to inform the Mayor that the General would not arrive till late the next day; the second to say that he was coming immediately and this again was shortly succeeded by a third announcing his actual arrival at the Governor's seat in Dorchester . . .

Boston presented a most animated scene, crowds of people in their best dresses were already moving through the streets, the military manoeuvering on the common and an immense cavalcade of citizens on horseback, among whom were two hundred truckmen dressed in their white frocks, who made a fine appearance. A barouche drawn by four white horses had previously been sent out to the Governor's seat for the General. At nine o'clock the procession moved and preceded by the City Authorities, who occupied a long train of carriages, the whole cavalcade advanced through Washington Street, and across the neck, to the lines of the city. Punctual to the appointed moment, they there met the General La Fayette, attended by his suite.

The Mayor then entered the barouche of the General, and the procession moved. At the moment La Fayette crossed the lines of the city, a signal was given, and a royal salute of one hundred and one guns was fired, every bell in the metropolis began to ring and the American standard was raised on the cupola of the State House and on Dorchester Heights. La Fayette advanced amid the acclamations of thousands, and during his triumphal progress through Boston, every street, every window, every balcony and every roof near which he passed, presented one mass of human beings, animated by one feeling, engaged in one object, and uniting in one general sentiment of enthusiasm.

The following day Lafayette attended commencement exercises at Cambridge and Miss Quincy recorded her impressions:

He paid the strictest attention to each of the speakers and whenever the tenor of an oration showed that a compliment was about to be paid to himself, he had a conscious apprehensive, yet pleased expression of countenance which seemed to say, "now it is coming."

Commencement Day at Harvard was a holiday. The banks were closed and business came to a standstill. Added to the usual merriment was Lafayette's presence in the city and the mere mention of his name caused the roaming crowds who had jammed into the city for a glimpse of the hero to go into an uproar.

The following day, August 26, Lafayette went again to Harvard College to attend a meeting of the Phi Beta Kappa Society. While there, someone remarked that he spoke the English language remarkably well. "And why should I not," Lafayette asked, "being an American just returned from a long visit to Europe?" The midday meal was served at Commons Hall and the day ended with a state banquet given by Governor Eustis.

Early on the morning of the twenty-seventh, carriages, an escort of cavalry, civil and military authorities, and a great number of citizens conveyed Lafayette to the Navy Yard at Charlestown. Commodore Bainbridge received the group there and after an inspection of the Yard the entourage ascended Bunker Hill. More speeches were given at the site of the historic battle and a luncheon was served under a huge tent. As was usual in most Lafayette celebrations, no women attended. Miss Quincy stayed at home:

This morning I employed a few hours of leisure in copying for the General my drawing of President Adams' house at Quincy, with a view of Boston, the State house and Dorchester Heights, decorated with the American standards in honor of his visit. At ten o'clock my father set off to accompany La Fayette to Charlestown and Bunker Hill; and in the course of the morning my mother called for Mrs. Ticknor and myself in our carriage, and we drove through the North part of the city and to Charlestown to see the decorations and inscriptions—When my father returned from Bunker Hill he gave me a curious relic of the battle, a button which had been worn on the 17th of June, 1775. It had apparently been broken, or shot off, and after remaining on the battlefield for nearly half a century, was found with several others by a gentleman of Charlestown, who gave one of them to La Fayette, and another to my father.

In the afternoon [Friday] I proceeded with my drawing and in the evening went to a splendid ball given by Mrs. Sears, in compliments to the General and other strangers in the city. At all these parties and indeed during the whole of La Fayette's visit, the ladies wore in compliment to him his picture engraved on white satin ribbon, tied round the arm or fastened to some part of the dress and some by way of variety stamped on their gloves.

There is little doubt that, during his stay in Boston, Lafayette was intent upon greeting personally as many citizens of the area as he could. On August 28 the *Boston Daily Advertiser* ran the following:

Notice—By request of Gen. LAFAYETTE the Committee of Arrangements inform their fellow citizens, who have not been introduced to him, that the General will be happy to receive them at the State House *this* day between the hours of 10 and 12.

In the afternoon Lafayette visited an encampment on Savin Hill and he was invited to try his skill at shooting. Much to the surprise of those present his shot knocked the floating target to pieces. After this Lafayette dined in Medford with ex-Governor Brooks and returned to Boston to attend a ball given by Senator Lloyd at his home on Somerset Street.

Lafayette had wisely expressed a wish to visit the Brattle Street Meeting House on Sunday and to sit in John Hancock's pew. "There

I used to attend the services of my good friend, Dr. Cooper, and I should feel strange in any other place of worship." Since all the congregations of Boston wanted the visitor as their guest this request solved a problem.

In the afternoon a sentimental reunion took place between Lafayette and his old friend John Adams, who lived in Quincy. It was necessary to break the Sabbath laws to make this journey, but there were few complaints. The former President was then eighty-nine years old and so feeble that, according to Levasseur, "he could not go out of his chamber, could scarcely raise himself from his chair, and his hands were unable to convey the food to his mouth without the pious assistance of his children or grandchildren."

In deference to John Adams' age and condition, Lafayette had requested that his visit should be unattended by any triumphal pomp. He traveled in a carriage accompanied by "two gentlemen of the city" and his son and Levasseur followed in a second carriage. On the way to Adams' residence Lafayette stopped at the country seat of the Quincy family, where he was introduced to the elderly members of the family who could not get into Boston for the festivities. Neighbors and tenants of the Quincys also were introduced. "La Fayette received them all very kindly," wrote the mayor's daughter, "and when my mother pointed out the badges they wore with his picture, [Lafayette] said with his usual graciousness, 'I am very much obliged to you.' "

Invitations continued to pour in from every area in the country and despite their busy schedule Levasseur and George Lafayette made plans for the weeks ahead. During this period in Boston Lafayette received a letter from Thomas Jefferson:

Really I am afraid that they will kill you with kindness, so many fine receptions I think must bring fatigue and use up your strength. . . . I see that you are to visit York-Town, my spirit will be on there with you; but I am too enfeebled by old age to make the journey; I do not walk outside of my garden. . . . I imagine that you will go to Charleston and Savannah.

What place is there that will not ask to take possession of you? Our village of Charlottesville insists upon receiving you, and would have claimed you as its guest, if in the neighborhood of Monticello you could be anybody's guest but mine.... Come, then, my dear friend, whenever it is convenient for you; make your headquarters here.... God bless and keep you; may He permit me to see you again and to embrace you!

Before he could continue his journey Lafayette had more Boston festivities to attend. On Monday, the thirtieth, a grand review of troops on Boston Common was held. The city troops had pitched their tents on the Common the night before and in the morning troops from surrounding areas marched into the city. Ladies viewed the spectacle from the windows of surrounding buildings. After the grand review a sham battle was held.

A luncheon then was served under tents on the Common for over twelve hundred people. The centerpieces were made up of relics of war materials picked up from the Bunker Hill battlefield. Lafayette took several pieces with him as a souvenir and Levasseur took one button as a reminder of the event. He remarked later in his book, "The care with which the Americans preserve and revere all the monuments of the revolution is very remarkable; everything which recalls this glorious epoch, is to them a precious relic, which they regard with almost religious fervor." In later years Americans would also revere any relic that represented Lafayette's tour of America.

Following the luncheon Lafayette held a reception in his rooms and in the evening attended a ball in his honor. During these last few days in Boston Miss Quincy recorded her impression of the General's son, George. Overshadowed by his father and the many honors bestowed upon him, Lafayette's son, smaller in stature than his father and already middle-aged, was infrequently given attention in the press or in eyewitness reports. Miss Quincy wrote:

During this visit short as it was I had more conversation with Washington La Fayette than I had ever had before. His appearance and manners are

17. *Above.* Music sheet for *Lafayette's March,* written especially for the General's review of troops in Boston on August 30, 1824. *Courtesy American Antiquarian Society*

18. *Right.* American artists who could not get Lafayette to sit for them copied his portrait from existing paintings. Panel in the Masonic Temple in Boston, by Edwin T. Billings, was adapted from earlier portrait by the French artist Amédée Geille. *Photograph Courtesy of State Street Bank and Trust Company, Boston*

not prepossessing but he improves on acquaintance and my father who has seen more of him than almost anyone else thinks he is not justly appreciated by people in general. Wherever he goes, everyone is so occupied with his father that they have little or no attention to bestow upon him. He told my mother today that he was really so affected by the scenes he witnessed and the manner in which he saw his father received, that he was forced continually to make great efforts to command his feelings.

On August 25 the *Bridgeport Courrier* printed a short description of father and son:

The General appears in fine health, of graceful figure and full six feet in stature; quite lame in his left leg, the effect of a wound he received in the war for our independence. His son is a man rather beneath the ordinary size, of a mild aspect, and of about 40 years.

The *Courrier* reporter was only too happy to attribute Lafayette's noticeable limp to sacrifices made in the cause of American liberty. In truth, his wound at the Battle of Brandywine had been slight but he had fallen on the ice in Paris in 1803 and broken his femur. A long and painful convalescence left him crippled and he walked with a cane.

Before Lafayette left the city of Boston he made a promise to return for ceremonies for the laying of a cornerstone for the proposed Bunker Hill monument. Throughout his tour this pledge was uppermost in his mind and by careful planning on the part of his son, his secretary, and helpful officials and citizens he was able to keep it.

6

TO NEW HAMPSHIRE AND BACK THROUGH WORCESTER AND HARTFORD

While in Boston Lafayette received a deputation from New Hampshire who invited him to visit the Navy Yard at Portsmouth. On Tuesday, August 31, Lafayette left Boston and, escorted by a troop of cavalry, stopped for a few minutes in Lexington, where he passed through two lines of militia to the base of the monument that had been erected to commemorate the famous battle. The entourage then commenced to Concord, where the citizens of the town were gathered on the village square and a tent of flowers had been erected. The young girls of Concord, crowned with wreaths of flowers, were gathered under the tent to serve refreshments to the General and his party. A long procession of citizens then followed Lafayette's carriage to Marblehead, where a mammoth breakfast was served. Although ceremonies in Marblehead delayed the procession considerably Lafayette did manage to reach the town of Salem by late afternoon, when he was served his third large meal of the day at a banquet held in Hamilton Hall.

The weather, which had behaved beautifully for the Boston festivities, stopped cooperating in Salem. In spite of a torrential rain every citizen of the town and several military corps turned out for the welcome. Numerous triumphal arches had been erected in the town and Lafayette entered the city on foot in order to be able to pass under them. Following a lengthy banquet, many toasts, and speeches, Lafayette left Salem to spend the night at Tracy's Inn, at Newburyport. The rain continued throughout the journey, but despite the weather and late hour of the General's arrival the citizens of Newburyport were not to be denied their opportunity to celebrate. Levasseur wrote, "The brilliance of the illumination and the fires lighted in appropriate places in the street, the shouts of the people, and the sight of armed troops advancing rapidly to the sound of the drum, might have led one to suppose we were entering a town taken by storm, and delivered to the flames!"

Upon his arrival in Portsmouth Lafayette was received by the usual delegation of town and state officials and corps of infantrymen. A thousand schoolchildren were lined up along the road in double file, and although it was still pouring, they wore on their heads only wreaths of flowers.

After a banquet Lafayette and his party were escorted to their lodgings in the house of the late Governor Langdon and on the way Levasseur stopped to observe the first American Indians he was to encounter on his tour. The secretary's curiosity was aroused to the point where some members of the committee induced a dozen or so of the Indians to visit him in his quarters so that he could study them further. The Indians had come down from the Canadian territory to exchange pelts for "toys and liquor." "I confess," wrote Levasseur, "that I found nothing in them which corresponded with my ideas of these children of nature. Their dresses had no other character than that of misery; crosses and chaplets had taken the place of their beautiful head-dresses of plumes, their furs and their arms; their drunken visages had nothing of that noble expression which is said so particularly to distinguish the savage man; at first their manners appeared affectionate, but it was soon evident that they were only servile or interested. They talked of beads and confession, as their fathers, no doubt, did of sorcerers and manitoes. In a word it appeared to me that these poor wretches had only changed superstitions, and that civilization had brought them its vices without any of its benefits."

After his tour of the Navy Yard and a banquet and ball, Lafayette traveled through the night to return to Boston and get a few hours sleep before leaving once again to go to Worcester. He passed through and stopped at West Cambridge, Lexington, and Concord and slept at Bolton. The next morning the citizens of Lancaster, Sterling, and West Boylston received him. On Friday, September 3, Lafayette was met at half past ten by officials of the city of Worcester. The *Worcester Spy* reporter described this reception:

Near the Worcester Bank the procession passed under several Flags extended across the street, from which appeared to be suspended the following motto—"*Hitherto I have only cherished your cause, NOW I go to serve it.*" This was the reply made by Gen. La Fayette when the American Commissioners endeavoured to dissuade him from embarking in the war of the revolution, because the gloomy aspect of affairs at that time [1776] almost destroyed the hope of final success.—Underneath was inscribed "BRANDYWINE, JAMESTOWN, VALLEYFORGE, YORK-TOWN." Soon after passing this, the General amidst cheers and welcomes uttered by thousands pressing around him, alighted at the gate of the spacious mansion house of Judge Lincoln, which had been thrown open for such ladies as chose to avail themselves of his hospitality to see the hero. Here language fails to do justice to the scene; each individual of a vast multitude seemed anxious to proclaim a hearty welcome to him who "not for the fading echoes of reknown, or purple robe of power," left a home, where he was rich in everything that endears life to man, to prop the sinking fortunes of our country. The gate and portico were decorated with evergreen and flags, and the windows, even to the upper story, were crowded with ladies greeting his approach with smiles and tears, while their handkerchiefs waved in token of welcome. Take it altogether, the effect was such it must be seen and felt to be realized.

Lafayette left Worcester at two in the afternoon and reached Stafford Springs late in the evening. The following morning he left that town and entered the city of Hartford, Connecticut, at eleven in the morning.

The mayor of Hartford delivered the welcoming address as the entire population of five thousand citizens watched. Lafayette was

19. Redware plate with "Lafayette" written in yellow slip. Probably made in Norwich, Connecticut. Many American potters made similarly decorated plates in celebration of visit. *Collection of William H. Guthman*

20. Printers published souvenir books for Lafayette's visit. Although this one appears to be the General's own "Memoirs," it was written by an anonymous author and material was taken from previously published books on Lafayette's life. *Benjamin DeForest Curtiss Collection, Watertown Library*

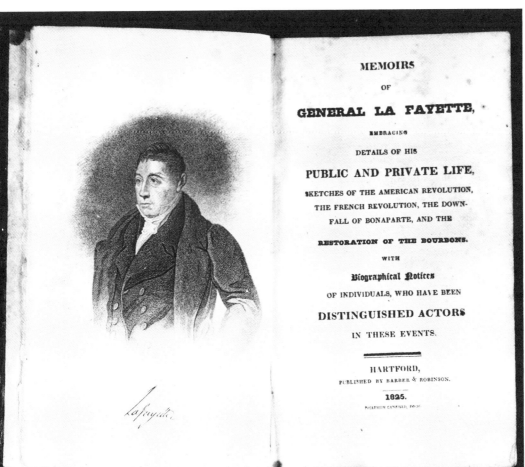

MEMOIRS

OF

GENERAL LA FAYETTE,

EMBRACING

DETAILS OF HIS

PUBLIC AND PRIVATE LIFE,

SKETCHES OF THE AMERICAN REVOLUTION,
THE FRENCH REVOLUTION, THE DOWN-
FALL OF BONAPARTE, AND THE

RESTORATION OF THE BOURBONS.

WITH

Biographical Notices

OF INDIVIDUALS, WHO HAVE BEEN

DISTINGUISHED ACTORS

IN THESE EVENTS.

HARTFORD,
PUBLISHED BY BARBER & ROBINSON.
1825.
PHILEMON CANFIELD, PRINT.

HONOR TO GEN. LAFAYETTE.

The following beautiful lines in honour of General LAFAYETTE, wer. written by Mrs. LYDIA L. SIGOURNEY, and presented by the Children of Hartford, who were decorated with Ribbons bearing the inscription "NOUS VOUS AIMONS LAFAYETTE." *

WELCOME thou to Freedom's clime,
Glorious Hero! Chief sublime!
Garlands bright for thee are **wreath'd**
Vows of filial ardour breath'd,
Vetran's cheeks with tears are **wet**,
" Nous vous aimons **LAFAYETTE**."

MONMOUTH'S field is rich with bloom,
Where thy warrior's found their tomb,
YORKTOWN'S heights resound no more,
Victor's shout or cannon's roar,
Yet our hearts record their debt,
" Nous vous aimons **LAFAYETTE**."

BRANDYWINE, whose current roll'd
Proud with blood of heroes bold,
That our Country's debt shall tell,

That our gratitude shall swell,
Infant breasts thy wounds regret,
" Nous vous aimons LAFAYETTE."

Sires, who sleep in glory's bed,
Sires, whose blood for us was shed,
Taught us when our knee we bend,
With the prayer thy name to blend:
Shall we e'er such charge forget?
No!—" Nous vous aimons LAFAYETTE.

When our blooming cheeks shall fade,
Pale with time, or sorrow's shade,
When our clustering tresses fair
Frosts of wintry age shall wear,
E'n till memory's sun be set,
" Nous vous aimons LAFAYETTE."

We love you Lafayette.

Printed by Henry Trumbull.

21. Poem written by Connecticut poet, Mrs. Lydia L. Sigourney, and recited by Hartford's school children to Lafayette during his visit to that city. Printed in black with colored wreath around portrait. Note Masonic emblem above Lafayette's head. *Collection of Donald Watt*

then escorted to the State House, where he received a welcoming address by Governor Wolcott. The General was then introduced to all citizens who could make their way into the crowded hall. Eight hundred schoolchildren waited outside to present the hero with a gold medal inscribed to commemorate the event. Afterward, as the procession passed the Hartford Institution for the Deaf and Dumb about sixty of the afflicted children were arranged in a line and held a huge banner inscribed, "What the nation expresses we feel." This was said to have affected Lafayette deeply.

A detachment of one hundred Revolutionary veterans escorted Lafayette to the steamboat *Oliver Ellsworth,* which would take him down the Connecticut River into Long Island Sound. The boat stopped for a reception in Middletown and it was not until seven that evening that the voyage continued downriver, reaching the Sound at daybreak.

Levasseur was impressed by its beauty and the handsome dwellings that adorned both banks. He remarked that while on the East River, whichever way he turned, he beheld beautiful country, houses, or farms.

The boat was expected by New Yorkers and even at that early hour the windows of the houses along the river banks were filled with people cheering and waving. The *Ellsworth* reached the city at noon, and although Lafayette had expected to enter the city quietly, the *Franklin,* a ship-of-the-line at anchor, fired a thirteen-gun salute. A huge crowd gathered on the wharf at Fulton Street and escorted the General to City Hotel. In the evening he attended a show of illuminations at the American Museum.

7

A RETURN TO NEW YORK

Lafayette had experienced the accolades and affection of thousands of Americans and described his impressions in a letter to his family that was probably written aboard the *Oliver Ellsworth:*

During a tour of six hundred miles, we have experienced all that can flatter or touch the human heart. In the midst of this continuous stream of emotions we experience a great pleasure when the name of La Grange appears on a triumphal arch or in a banquet hall. I am counting on Levasseur and on George, to give you the details of all these fairy scenes. I have found more old soldiers of the Revolution than I had expected, and it has been sweet to see what memories I had left in their hearts—I have the satisfaction of thinking that my presence has affected many reconciliations between political parties; men, who have not spoken to one another for more than twenty years, have made arrangements together and have invited one another to entertainments in our honour, and revive together common memories of the Revolution. I acquit myself as little badly as possible under the obligations, often unexpected, of answering to discourses in the middle of a multitude of hearers, who luckily are kindly disposed and find my accent hardly perceptible, and my English excellent. It would not be so in the streets of London; but here everything gets by, thanks to kindliness.

Lafayette's schedule was no less busy on his second visit to New York than it had been after his arrival. On Monday, September 6, he visited Columbia College in the morning accompanied by the mayor and Colonel Nicholas Fish. It was Lafayette's sixty-seventh birthday and the Society of the Cincinnati of New York had asked for the honor of entertaining him that evening. At four in the afternoon a long double file of elderly men, all former officers of the American army, arrived at the City Hotel. Levasseur described the pairs of old soldiers as "holding each other by the arm for the sake of mutual support." They were preceded by a military band and found it difficult to march in time to the music.

A decoration of the Order of the Cincinnatus, which had been worn by George Washington, was attached to Lafayette's button-hole and the march of the aged veterans commenced to Washington Hall, where a banquet was prepared. The hall was decorated with sixty banners bearing the names of heroes of the Revolution who were deceased and toward the conclusion of the dinner a curtain was drawn to reveal a large allegorical transparency of Washington and Lafayette holding each other by the hand before the altar of Liberty and receiving a civic wreath from the hands of America. Following the final course of an elaborate dinner and many toasts the order of the day at Yorktown on the seventeenth of October 1781 was read and followed by prolonged applause and three loud cheers. After this a ballad composed in 1792 describing Lafayette's accomplishments and his imprisonment in Olmütz was sung. This song had been very popular in the United States and was instrumental in arousing American sympathy for Lafayette's plight.

By this time American industries had had time to manufacture souvenir commemoratives for use in towns and cities Lafayette was to visit. In addition, the manufacturers and craftsmen vied with one another to make presentation gifts to Lafayette that would represent the best that American citizens could produce in the first quarter of the nineteenth century. If it could be arranged, it was all to the good if something made to be presented to the illustrious guest was outstanding enough to receive some press notice.

A short article appeared as early as August 19, 1824, in the *Commercial Advertiser,* of New York, that seemed to set a precedent to

22. Very rare embossed paper doily or place mat with engraved portrait of Lafayette by P. Maverick, 342 Broadway, New York. Possibly used at Lafayette's sixty-seventh birthday dinner. *Courtesy American Antiquarian Society*

23. Bronze medal struck for Lafayette's visit to America in 1824. Obverse, Lafayette's profile. Marked "Caunois French." *Collection of William H. Guthman*

24. Reverse of Lafayette medal. Inscribed "The Defender/of American and/French Liberty./1777–1824./Born in Chavaniac/The 6 September/1757." *Collection of William H. Guthman*

ensure that gifts made expressly for Lafayette would be given attention in the newspapers and other periodicals of the day:

Messrs. Martinet and Roe, umbrella manufacturers of this city, have made a superb umbrella, to be presented to the marquis as a token of their respect for his character and services. It is one of the patent kind, the shaft of beautiful curl maple and mounted with fine ivory and gold. It is not the intrinsic value of such presents that constitutes their worth, but the feelings of the hearts that prompt them.

Another gift made especially for Lafayette that would bring attention to an American industry was a set of presentation buttons struck in solid gold. The buttons were made by the firm of Leavenworth, Hayden, and Scovill, of Waterbury, Connecticut, which had been in the button manufacturing business since 1811. The buttons were not presented to Lafayette until shortly before his return to France, but the following article appeared in *Nile's Register,* of New York, as early as October 23, 1824:

We have seen at Mr. Ladd's, 30 Wall Street, a lump of pure gold, found in Mecklenburg County, S. C. [later changed to North Carolina in an editorial note] which has been sold by Mr. Ladd for the purpose of making a set of buttons for La Fayette, to bear the likeness of Washington.

On July 7, 1825, an announcement appeared in the *New York Gazette:*

We yesterday saw at Mr. Ladd's watch store in Wall Street, a set of Buttons, with the head of Washington on them, manufactured of North Carolina Gold, and intended as a present to General Lafayette. They were manufactured by Mess Hayden, Scofield and Levenger, of Connecticut, and afford another example of the skill of American artists.

Although the reporter did not record the firm's name correctly, he at least attracted attention to the product. In all, seventeen buttons were struck in solid gold, fourteen of which were given to Lafayette and one each to the three partners of the firm. Each of the partners lost his button and for many years nothing was known of the set given to the nation's guest. In 1956 the top floor of Lafayette's chateau, La Grange, was opened after having been sealed for one hundred and twenty years, revealing many letters, papers, books, and relics of Lafayette's trip to America. Among these artifacts were ten of the buttons made in Waterbury. They have been placed on display at La Grange, which is now a museum dedicated to Lafayette memorabilia.

The Lafayette button with Washington's profile was accompanied by the production of a commercial product made by the same manufacturer to be sold to the public as a commemorative of the visit. Once it was announced that the solid gold buttons were being made, Leavenworth, Hayden, and Scovill produced buttons with Lafayette's profile that were struck in brass. The *New York Commercial Advertiser* on October 1824 and January 1825 ran the following notice:

LA FAYETTE BUTTONS
A NEW AND ELEGANT ARTICLE

Campfield offers to the public another Capital Likeness of Gen. La Fayette stamped upon Buttons of several sizes—extra rich gilt. They were manufactured by Leavenworth, Hayden & Scovill, of Connecticut, and will be sold in quantities to suit purchasers. The likeness was executed by C. C. Wright (Durand and Wright), from a plaster cast, taken a few weeks ago by Mr. Frazer, which is pronounced by artists to be very superior.

Boys' Clothing Emporiaum
303 Broadway, corner of Duane St.

Many manufacturers capitalized on the great fervor of patriotism brought about by Lafayette's visit and made souvenirs that would appeal to popular taste. It is most doubtful that many of the plans for these products were made much before the General finished his first tour through New England. By the time he had returned to New York he had already accepted invitations from all

We yesterday saw at Mr Ladd's watch store in Wall street, a set of Buttons, with the head of Washington on them, manufactured of North Carolina Gold, and intended as a present to General Lafayette. They were manufactured by Mess Hayden, Scofield and Levenger, of Connecticut, and afford another example of the skill of American artists.

NEW YORK GAZETTE
July 7, 1825

25. Notice from *New York Gazette,* July 7, 1825, tells of display of gold buttons before presentation to Lafayette. *Mattatuck Museum*

26. Gold button with profile of Washington made for Lafayette in Waterbury, Connecticut. *Mattatuck Museum*

27. Reverse of gold presentation button reads, "Presented to General Lafayette by L. H. Scovill, Button Manufacturers, Waterbury, Con." This design has been reproduced in brass several times through firm's long history. *Mattatuck Museum*

LA FAYETTE BUTTONS.
A NEW AND ELEGANT ARTICLE.
CAMPFIELD offers to the public *another Capital Likeness of Gen. La Fayette* stamped upon Buttons of several sizes—extra rich gilt. They were manufactured by Leavenworth, Hayden & Scovill, of Connecticut, and will be sold in quantities to suit purchasers. The likeness was executed by C. C. Wright, (Durand & Wright,) from a plaster cast, taken a few weeks ago by Mr. Frazer, which is pronounced by artists to be very superior.
Boys' Clothing Emporium,
oct 8   303 Broadway, corner of Duane-st.

28. Advertisement from *New York Commercial Advertiser,* October 1824 and January 1825. Announces Lafayette profile buttons made in Waterbury, Connecticut, as souvenirs of visit. *Mattatuck Museum*

29. Lafayette medallion button was made in brass in three sizes, but head was same size on all of them. *Mattatuck Museum*

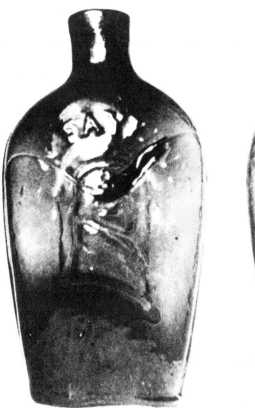

30. (*a and b*) Lafayette whiskey flask, made by Mount Vernon Glass Works, is dark yellow-green and has Masonic devices on reverse. *Mattatuck Museum*

the important eastern cities and the scope of his presence in the United States had been felt. Elaborate plans were being made for receptions, and popular demand for anything with Lafayette's likeness caused many manufacturers to look for ways of stimulating their businesses by producing "Lafayette" products.

In a year of what promised to be wild celebration in the nation whiskey flasks were a fitting medium for Lafayette's likeness and molds were made almost simultaneously with the landing of the *Cadmus*. One bottle manufacturer who lost no time in producing souvenir flasks was Dr. Dyott, of Philadelphia. The September 10, 1824, issue of the *United States Gazette* carried the following advertisement:

LA FAYETTE FLASKS. Pint pocket Bottles, with the likeness of General La Fayette, and on the reverse the United States Coat of Arms, are now blowing at the Kensington Glass Works, and for sale at the N. E. corner of Second and Race streets, where orders will be received and executed at the shortest notice by Sept. 10. T. W. Dyott.

Other glass manufacturers who made flasks to commemorate Lafayette's visit were the Coventry (Connecticut) Glass Works, Knox and McKee in Wheeling, West Virginia, and the Mount Vernon Glass Works. Lafayette's portrait was used in conjunction with De Witt Clinton, Masonic symbols, Washington's portrait, and other patriotic symbols and devices.

The souvenirs that could be produced the most quickly were ephemeral items that were printed. Round papier mâché snuff boxes with engraved paper labels pasted on the lids showing the "Landing of the Cadmus" appeared early on the market. Apparently, the copyright of the engravings were poor protection for the artists, for designs were pirated almost as soon as the originals appeared.

Ironically, the manufacturers who seemed to profit the most from the sale of Lafayette commemoratives were the potters of Staffordshire, England. Using existing portraits of Lafayette as

31. Lafayette flask has Masonic devices on reverse. "T. S." stands for Thomas Stebbins of Coventry, Connecticut, Glass Works. Dark amber color. *Mattatuck Museum*

32. Lafayette flask made by Coventry Glass Works has name of town misspelled in mold. Reverse is liberty cap on pole, stars, and "S & S," for Stebbins and Stebbins. Dark amber glass. *Mattatuck Museum*

33. Platter showing full front view of La Grange, Lafayette's estate in France. Printed in dark blue. Made by Enoch Wood & Sons, Staffordshire, England, in 1825. *Mattatuck Museum*

34. Staffordshire plate showing east view of La Grange. Printed in dark blue. Made by Enoch Wood & Sons. Although these plates were first made in 1825 they were popular in America for some years after Lafayette's visit. *Mattatuck Museum*

models for engravings, they made plates, plaques, and jugs that welcomed Lafayette to America's shores. In addition to the portrait tableware and souvenir pottery, plates and platters were made decorated with views of La Grange. Lafayette's portrait also was used as border decoration for plates that had American or sometimes even British views in the center. All of these Lafayette plates and many others with scenes of America and portraits of other patriots were made and sold for years following Lafayette's visit to America.

Souvenirs closely associated with the actual presence of Lafayette were the white ribbons engraved by local printers in towns where Lafayette receptions were held. These were worn by the troops and arrangement committees, town or state officials, or by the multitudes who turned out to see the hero. They were sold by either the printers, themselves, or local stores.

Thus, by the time Lafayette was back in New York, touring forts, public schools, almshouses, orphan asylums, hospitals and insane asylums, the Academy of Arts, and the Free School for Young Africans, he must have seen his own image everywhere he turned. He was the guest at two New York theater productions presented in his honor. A gala performance of *The Siege of Yorktown* was held at the Park Theater on the evening of Wednesday, September 8, and on the next night Lafayette saw a performance of *Lafayette, or the Hero of Olmütz*. Neither performance was seen as originally produced, because when the hero appeared in the theaters the tumult was so loud and prolonged that it was impossible for the actors to continue in their parts. Instead they sang some verses from "The Companion of Washington," "The Captive of Olmütz," or "The Guest of the Nation." Composers and lyricists had been as busy as the manufacturers in providing suitable material for the many entertainments.

Lafayette's visit coincided with the construction of the Erie Canal and this event was tied in with many of the celebrations in Lafayette's honor. On Saturday, September 11, Lafayette was a

35. Lafayette's portrait on Liverpool jug. Note name above portrait is spelled "Fayitte," an error of British engravers. Made by Richard Hall & Son, 1825–32. Reverse is portrait of Washington. *Photograph from Catalogue de L'Exposition, Le Général La Fayette, Paris, Mai, 1934.*

36. Liverpool jug, also made by Richard Hall & Son, is probably later than jug in previous photograph and has corrected spelling of name above portrait. Glaze is improved also. Reverse is portrait of Benjamin Franklin. *Mr. and Mrs. I. J. Zweig*

37. Earthenware plaque, cream-colored glaze, with portrait of Lafayette printed in black. Made in England by Richard Hall & Son. Portrait is adapted from Ary Sheffer painting. *Collection of Jan and Larry Malis*

38. *Below.* Staffordshire platter, printed in blue, around 1825. Inscribed "General La Fayette/ Welcome to the Land of Liberty. He was born at Auvergne in France in 1757 Joined the American Struggle/in 1777 In 1784 he returned to France loaded with the honours and gratitude of/the American people he returned in the Cadamus [sic] to New York Augt 13th 1824." *Collection of Jan and Larry Malis*

39. Staffordshire plate, blue feather edge, sepia center print of Lafayette and Washington. *Collection of William H. Guthman*

40. Staffordshire plate, made around 1825, by J. and R. Clews. Embossed border with blue rim, blue medallion portrait in center. *Mattatuck Museum*

41. Pitcher, printed in dark blue, with legend "Welcome Lafayette, the Nations Guest and our Country's Glory," was made by British potters for American market around 1825. *Collection of William H. Guthman*

guest of the Masonic celebration of the Knights Templar. A great banquet was given in the late afternoon on the same day by the French citizens of New York and the decorations brought attention to the coincidence of the two great events, Lafayette's visit and the completion of the canal, occurring that year in America. The table almost filled the length of the room, in Washington Hall. It was eighty feet long and six feet wide, and the centerpiece, which ran the entire length of the table, was a miniature replica of the Erie Canal, made of sheet lead and surrounded by fresh green moss. The leaden tube, which curved to conform to the contours of the canal, was filled with water on which floated tiny canal boats. Islands, forests, excavations, tunnels, bridges, and rocks were all realistically in place. Mountains surrounded a miniature replica of the town of Lockport, New York.

"This 75 feet of canal, contrasted with white table-cloths," wrote one reporter, "all along the whole length, plates, knives, and forks, sparkling cut decanters, with wine-glasses, tumblers, &c. all formed a most beautiful appearance: but more especially when the whole number of the immense glass lamps were put into illumination, the whole *coup d'oeil* commanded every body's admiration."

Although it always seemed possible for various groups to manage large and elaborate entertainments for Lafayette upon rather short notice, the major event given by the citizens of New York had been planned for weeks before the *Cadmus* landed. This party was to take place at Castle Garden, in the Battery, which was a public park. The structure in which the major events were to be held was a circular fort about two hundred feet in diameter. A three-hundred-foot bridge connected the fort to the Battery.

Although Levasseur in his book reported the Castle Garden fête as having been held on Monday, contemporary newspapers prove that the secretary's memory for dates was often faulty and the event actually occurred on the following day. However, his description of the event was probably much more dependable:

We went there in the evening by the light of an illumination, we found the bridge covered with rich carpets from one end to the other, and on each side bordered with a line of beautiful green trees. In the middle of the bridge arose a pyramid sixty-five feet high, illuminated with coloured lamps, surmounted by a brilliant star in the centre of which blazed the name of Lafayette. Notwithstanding the magnificence of the entry, our surprise and admiration were strongly augmented on entering the circle of the fort. The hall, about six hundred feet in circumference, around which was a vast amphitheatre, containing nearly six thousand persons. An arch formed of the flags of all nations mingled with symmetry and elegance. Over the principal entrance was a triumphal arch of flowers, surmounted by a colossal statue of Washington, resting upon two pieces of cannon. In the centre stood the genius of America, having on a shield these words, "TO THE NATION'S GUEST". In front of the gate raised upon a platform was a richly decorated marquee, ornamented with a bust of Hamilton; in front were two pieces of cannon taken at Yorktown. The marquee was intended for Lafayette. Around the hall thirteen columns, bore the arms of the first states of the confederation. This space was illuminated by a thousand torches, the brilliance of which was reflected by numerous stands of arms.

Upon Lafayette's entry the band struck up "See the Conquering Hero Comes" and as he sat down in the chair of honor the cloths that surrounded and enclosed the hall were raised to reveal the scene to the people on boats of a variety of sizes and types that had gathered around the Battery. It was a beautiful moonlit night and the "thousand torches" made the scene visible for miles.

The highlight of the evening followed shortly thereafter. In front of Lafayette's chair a grand transparency was suddenly uncovered and presented an exact picture of La Grange with its fine Gothic towers. The inscription "Here is His Home" was written below it. Dancing followed this dramatic event for which special music had been written and Lafayette talked and shook hands with everyone who could get close to him. The *New York Evening Post* reported, "We hazard nothing in saying it was the most magnificent fête under cover in the world. . . . It was a festival that realizes all that we read of in the Persian tales or Arabian Nights,

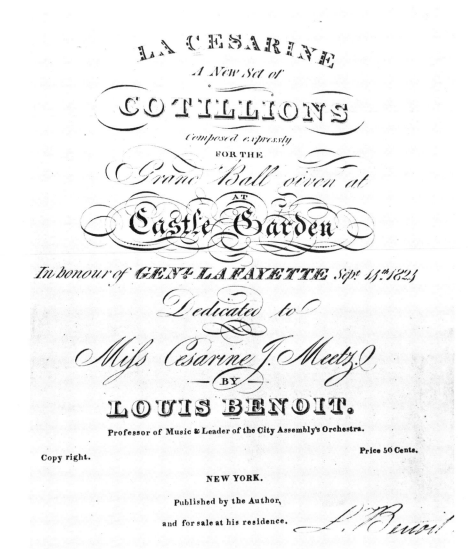

42. Cover of special music written in honor of Lafayette and played at celebration at Castle Garden. *Courtesy American Antiquarian Society*

which dazzled the eye and bewildered the imagination."

This was Lafayette's last night in New York on this segment of his tour. The celebration continued until around two in the morning, when the steamboat *James Kent* arrived to convey Lafayette and his party up the Hudson River for a visit to Albany. As many citizens of New York as would fit on the boat piled onto the deck along with the New York Committee of Arrangements. Levasseur wrote of the departure, "We soon lost sight of Castle Garden, and instead of the joyous sounds of music, we heard nothing but the monotonous noise of the steam machinery struggling against the rapid waves of the Hudson."

8

A TRIP UP THE
HUDSON RIVER

During the Castle Garden fête Lafayette said farewell to Captain Allyn, who was departing on the *Cadmus* for another voyage to France. He was to take mail from the travelers to the family at La Grange, and Lafayette had written a letter home on September 13:

I am touched to the quick by marks of affection, and when I see deputations from all points in the United States, from cities and villages come to invite me, after all that traveling, to pass an hour with them, when I see men and women come two hundred miles to shake my hand for a moment, should I not feel ashamed not to write answers to all the addresses, or do no more than barely greet people that come to see me, or to be unable to say whether I shall pass such a spot, especially when I am aware of all the expenses and inconveniences they have incurred in order to welcome me? I do the best I can.... Everything is enchanting, but I feel that I shall enjoy our beloved family circle more than ever.

In spite of the high excitement that caused such a large group of New York's citizens to squeeze aboard the *James Kent,* it was soon realized that it had been a mistake to allow this to have happened. The sleeping arrangements that had been carefully made by the committee had to be abandoned. There were so many women present that berths were given up to them and Auguste Levasseur, the General, and his son, George, shared a stateroom with General Lewis and Colonel Fish. The rest of the men were forced to sleep on deck. It is doubtful whether many slept at all that night, since every few minutes, as the *James Kent* passed towns along the banks of the Hudson River, cannon were fired to announce the presence of Lafayette. In addition, the boat became grounded on an oyster bank shortly before dawn and the efforts of the crew to free it caused more excitement and noise. By this time everyone was on deck to view the majestic banks of the Hudson.

Once free, the *James Kent* chugged along at the fast rate of ten miles an hour, despite the fact that it was overloaded and going against the current. Lafayette passed the time on deck talking over old times with a group of Revolutionary soldiers. Upon sighting the house in which Benedict Arnold had sold out to the enemy there was much conversation about the traitor and his motivations.

The first important stop for the party was at West Point, where Lafayette reviewed the cadet corps of two hundred students and was given a tour of the school. At six o'clock the party returned to the *Kent* and at this time a large part of the passengers boarded another boat that would take them back to New York. The *Kent* then left to arrive in Newburgh, New York, where thirty thousand people had been waiting since three that afternoon to welcome the nation's guest.

A torchlight parade escorted Lafayette to the hotel, where tables had been set since early that morning, but when word was passed among the citizens of Newburgh that Lafayette planned to leave as soon as the banquet was over, the first and only near-riot during his entire visit took place outside the hotel. There were loud complaints that the late hour of his arrival had given few citizens a chance to see the hero and there were cries that he must not leave until sunrise, when he could bestow his benediction on the children of the town. As the crowd threatened to become a problem, the mayor of Newburgh took Lafayette onto the balcony of the hotel and addressed the people: "Gentlemen, do you wish to distress the nation's guest?" There were cries of "No! No!"

"Do you wish that Lafayette should be deprived of his liberty, in a country indebted to him for its freedom?" The answer was the same.

"Then listen to what I am about to say, and do not force me to call upon the law to restore order." The silence, according to contemporary accounts, became "profound."

"Your friend is expected at Albany, he is engaged to be there tomorrow before evening; he has already been delayed for three hours by an unexpected accident; if you retain him here until tomorrow, you will deprive him of the pleasure of visiting all the other towns which expect him upon his passage, and you will make him break all his engagements; do you wish to give him this pain?" The good citizens of Newburgh screamed "NO! NO! NO!" to this question. Lafayette then addressed the crowd and this silenced the dissenters.

The major problem, apparently, was that a huge ball had been prepared for the evening's entertainment. New dresses had been made and the children scrubbed and promised the blessings of the hero. Now all the women and children of the town were gathered in a hall and had not even seen the General, whose hasty retreat would deprive them of an expensive celebration that had been planned for days. Lafayette, upon being told this, made a brief appearance at the hall, where he was showered with wreaths and flowers. The men of the town then quickly formed a double row from the hall to the river's edge, and after receiving greetings from each man as he passed through the line, Lafayette boarded the *James Kent* once again and was on his way. The grand ball of Newburgh went on without him.

At dawn on Thursday, September 16, the *James Kent* steamed into Poughkeepsie, where the wharves and shore were crowded with soldiers, citizens, and "even a great number of ladies," who had waited up all night for a glimpse of Lafayette. Breakfast, a reception, and a procession were held.

The next stop for the General was for a visit to the family of General Morgan, who resided on the right bank of the Hudson

above Poughkeepsie in Staatsburg. At four o'clock the party disembarked at Clermont, the home of Robert L. Livingston, where they
were entertained by a review of the militia, a procession of the
Masonic fraternities of the vicinity, and a ball in the evening.

The citizens of the town of Catskill were to be hosts to Lafayette
for a few brief moments during which he conversed with some
Revolutionary soldiers, one of whom he recognized as having
fought with him at Brandywine. A detachment of eighty old soldiers waited for Lafayette at the little town of Hudson, across the
river from Catskill. Elaborate plans had been made, the usual triumphal arches built, and public entertainments prepared, but Lafayette had to skip the whole event in order to get to Albany in time.
The *Kent* now was making only six miles an hour against a strong
current and it was five o'clock when the boat reached Overslaugh,
a short distance from its destination. There the voyage had to be
suspended because the steamboat was drawing too much water.
Lafayette and the others were placed in barouches and given an
escort of dragoons. The hero thus was conveyed to the town of
Greenbush, where another triumphal arch had been erected and
under which refreshments were served and speeches made.

It wasn't until nightfall of Friday, September 17, that Lafayette
arrived across the river from Albany. The carriages were placed
aboard a steamboat called a "horse's back" and were drawn across
the river. The incessant discharge of cannons caused the horses to
rear, and George, afraid that the horses would pull the carriages
overboard, left his own carriage to hold the horses of his father's.

At the entrance to Albany a procession was formed amidst the
thick crowd that waited at the river bank. A triumphal arch, built
at the start of the route the procession would take, was topped by
a huge stuffed and somehow mechanized eagle that flapped its
wings as Lafayette passed through the arch. High pyramids of
blazing wood illuminated the streets along the route. The procession stopped at the capitol building, where the galleries were
filled with Albany's female population. A welcoming address by

43. Letter dated September 11, 1824, and written in Catskill, New York, to muster troops for Lafayette's visit:

By the enclosed notice you will perceive that *General La Fayette* will visit this village on Thursday morning next. We should be happy to have all the *Uniformed Troops* in the country join in paying honours to the *General*—to do which it will be necessary that they be here, or near here on *Wednesday evening*, as he is expected to arrive *early* in the morning. We trust you will use every exertion to give the necessary information and to get out the troops.

Collection of William H. Guthman

44. Troops also were mustered in Athens, New York, on the Hudson River, above Catskill. Undated letter from Col. Edmund, 47th Infantry, to Capt. John Forbes reads:

La Fayette is expected to visit this City in the course of next week and the uniform Company of the 47th regt will be called out to the occasion. We should be very happy to be honored with your company in procession on the occasion. The precise time of his visit is not yet known. When it is will communicate the same to you. In the mean time, if you conclude to accept our invitation you can hold your Company in readiness to parade at a moments warning.

I would be pleased to have you answer, as early as possible when I will forward you the order of arrangements.

Collection of William H. Guthman

the mayor was given to which Lafayette replied by telling of the wilderness that had been Albany not a half century before. He expressed his congratulations to its citizens for the growth and prosperity that were now evident.

From the senate chamber the group went to the apartments of Governor Joseph C. Yates, who received Lafayette in the name of the state. Lafayette then was conducted to a balcony of the capitol and was presented to the crowds assembled in the streets below. At the moment when Lafayette advanced between the two central columns of the balcony another stuffed eagle swooped down and placed a crown of laurels and evergreens upon his head. As reported by Levasseur, "This was loudly applauded by the numerous spectators."

The day at Albany was described by Lafayette's secretary as one "under which a man less robust than Lafayette must have sunk," and the festivities terminated in a supper after which toasts were drunk to the health of the nation's guest and "to the liberty and sovereignty of the people." A ball was held in the assembly chamber of the capitol and Lafayette left at midnight to seek some welcome rest.

Levasseur's impressions of the city of Albany in 1824 were somewhat mixed. "With the exception of the capitol building," he wrote, "there is no building which has a monumental aspect." Regardless of its architectural deficiencies the city of Albany at that time was extremely busy and commercially successful. The near-completion of the Erie Canal system promised the city an even brighter future. In 1824 about twenty-four steamboats plied continuously between New York City and Albany and both cities prospered.

On the morning of Saturday, September 18, while De Witt Clinton awarded Lafayette with a diploma making him a member of the Literary and Philosophical Society of New York, a huge procession was forming outside Lafayette's hotel that would escort him to the edge of the canal that led to Troy. Five canal boats were placed at the disposal of the party. The first carried a band of

45. Lafayette ribbon from Albany has short history of hero's career and account of his historic visit to that city. *Collection of Jan and Larry Malis*

46. "Welcome La Fayette, the Nation's Guest." White silk ribbon engraved by Myron King of Troy, New York. *De Witt Collection, University of Hartford*

musicians; the second, Lafayette, George, Auguste, Governor Yates, ex-Governors Lewis and Clinton, the mayor and the city council; and the last three carried a military escort composed of an artillery company and three companies of infantry.

Troy was sighted before noon, at the point where the canal runs into the Hudson River, and General Lafayette was astonished at the sight of the city. "What!" he cried, "This town has arisen as if by enchantment!" He explained that in 1778, when he had crossed the Hudson at this point, there were only a few scattered cabins at the site of a city that now boasted eight thousand inhabitants.

The people of Troy had arranged the usual procession, led by the members of the local Masonic lodges, and a breakfast, after which the General reviewed the local troops. He also visited Mrs. Emma Willard's female seminary, where the young ladies, all attired in white dresses, sang for him. After another full day Lafayette returned to Albany in the evening and reembarked on the *James Kent.*

Huge bonfires on the banks of the Hudson signaled Lafayette's departure from Albany. The descension of the Hudson was much easier and faster than the trip up the river. Short stops were made at Newburgh, West Point, and a few other small villages and in thirty-six hours Lafayette was back in New York at Van Cortlandt wharf. At his own request all public entertainments for his few remaining days in New York were dispensed with so that he could spend some time with old friends. Nevertheless, there were certain commitments already made and on Monday, September 20, he dined as the guest of the Freemasons of the city and attended the Park Theater in the evening, where he saw Mr. Barnes as "Sir Peter Teazle" in *School for Scandal.* He also attended an exhibition of fireworks and a balloon ascension at Castle Garden.

On Wednesday, September 23, the *New York American* reported the following:

47. A song, "Massa Georgee Washington and General Lafayette" was performed at Chatham Gardens Theatre in New York. Song was copyright in October 1824. *Courtesy American Antiquarian Society*

General Lafayette left us this morning. Fortunate and happy as our city has been in possessing him so long; and though every inhabitant in it, probably, who could make the effort, has, on some of the numerous occasions in which he presented himself to the public, approached and seen, if not spoken to him, yet the interest at the moment of his departure was as unabated and zealous as on his first arrival.

9

THROUGH NEW JERSEY TO PHILADELPHIA

New York was saddened by Lafayette's departure. Once more a crowd filled the streets to say farewell to him. "At present," wrote Levasseur, "not one cry of joy, not one acclamation." Although Lafayette had expressed a wish to walk to the steamboat that awaited him, his decision soon was found to have been unwise because of the crowds that pressed upon him. People reached out to touch him, to shake his hand, and some even threw themselves in his path. However, the sadness was soon forgotten as the *James Kent* crossed the river to the New Jersey shore, where a jubilant crowd awaited the arrival of Lafayette in their state. The governor of the state, Isaac H. Williamson, received Lafayette at Lyon's Hotel in Jersey City and, with a detachment of militia, accompanied the General through Bergen and into Newark. The final reception for the day was held in Elizabeth at River's Hotel and Lafayette spent the night at the residence of General Dayton.

The following day, Friday, September 24, the entourage proceeded through Rahway and Woodbridge to New Brunswick. Travel was slow because there were receptions and speeches in every town and upon reaching New Brunswick there was a banquet and gala ball at Follett's Old Bell Hotel. By this time, Lafayette's schedule had been carefully worked out with a skill that would rival the most competent political advance men of today.

On the following day Lafayette was received by the citizens of Kingston and at Newark the nation's guest was hailed by patriotic songs sung by a huge chorus of children. Upon his arrival at Princeton, Lafayette was received by the faculty, students, and president of the college, attended a luncheon, and left at twelve-thirty to proceed to Trenton. He was given many gifts along the way, one of which, a cane with a golden head, had sentimental attachments. The wood was made from a branch of an apple tree under which he had breakfasted with Washington when he passed through Bergen, New Jersey, during the Revolution. The entire area through which he was passing was of sentimental interest for him. It reminded him of Washington's retreat and offensive at Trenton and Princeton in 1776.

The twenty-sixth of September was a Sunday and Lafayette attended services at the Presbyterian church of Trenton. The previous night's festivities, a reception by three thousand militia, a procession through Trenton's main streets, a welcome by the mayor, and a dinner with the Revolutionary veterans of the city had made a relatively quiet Sunday a welcome relief. Following church services Lafayette went in a carriage with the governor and one of his aides to Bordentown to visit Joseph Bonaparte, the former king of Spain, who was in exile in the United States.

On Monday Lafayette crossed the Delaware over a remarkable wooden bridge that was ample enough to have a sidewalk and accommodate two-way traffic. At his entrance into Pennsylvania Lafayette was greeted by Governor John Andrew Shulze, his staff, and a sizable number of militia and civilians. After breakfast in Morrisville, the militia escorted the party to Bristol and a ball was held in the evening at Holmesburg. Lafayette spent the night at the arsenal at Frankfort. He would need all the rest he could get for his march into Philadelphia on the following day.

On Tuesday, September 28, the large body of troops that had gathered at the arsenal formed the beginning of what would be a huge procession. In Levasseur's words, "As we approached Philadelphia the footmen, horsemen, and carriages, increased our procession so much, that we could not, without great difficulty advance. On a plain at a short distance from the city, General Lafayette was received by the civil and military officers, and about 6000 uniformed militia." The line of march started at Rush's Field, near Kensington, and proceeded at noon into the city.

Philadelphia had had time to make elaborate plans for Lafayette's visit and was determined not to be outdone by Boston or New York. The entire population of the city and surrounding areas had come out for the spectacle and scaffolding had been erected on each side of the streets through which the procession was to pass. There is no way to understand the scope of the Philadelphia celebration without seeing the planned order of procession:

1. A cavalcade of one hundred citizens, mounted.

2. One hundred field and staff officers, mounted.

3. Sixty cavalry, in the form of a hollow square.

4. A band of musicians, mounted.

5. A corps of one hundred and sixty cavalry.

6. A detachment of artillery, with four pieces of ordnance.

7. A brigade of infantry, of near two thousand men, including one or two companies of riflemen, all in uniform.

8. The committee of arrangements, all in carriages.

9. General Lafayette, accompanied by Judge Peters, in a barouche, with six cream-colored horses, outriders in livery, mounted on horses of the same color.

10. Governor Shulze and suite, in a barouche and four brown horses.

11. Governor Williamson, of New Jersey, and suite in a like carriage and brown horses.

12. Two other barouches, with distinguished individuals.

13. One hundred and fifty Revolutionary heroes, drawn in three cars of great magnitude, with four horses each, trimmed with white and red, and the cars decorated with evergreens, flags, and emblematical descriptions, and each soldier wearing the Revolutionary cockade. On the side of the first car, written in large gold

letters, were the words "Defenders of our Country"; on the other, "The Survivors of 1776"; in front, "Washington"; and in the rear, "Lafayette."

14. A large car containing a body of printers, and also the various articles belonging to a printing office. The compositors and pressmen were at work, and the latter distributed at intervals an ode prepared for the occasion by Alderman Barker. The members of the Typographical Society followed, preceded by a banner inscribed with "Lafayette, the Friend of Universal Liberty and the Rights of the Press."

15. A body of four hundred young men of the city and the County of Philadelphia.

16. Two hundred cordwinders, with banners, badges, and other emblems.

17. Three hundred weavers.

18. One hundred and fifty ropemakers.

19. One hundred and fifty young boys.

20. One hundred shipbuilders.

21. Seven hundred mechanics of different branches of trade.

22. One hundred and fifty coopers, preceded by a car containing a cooper's shop, with workmen fitting staves, driving hoops, and performing other cooper's tasks.

23. One hundred and fifty butchers, well mounted and handsomely dressed and ornamented.

24. Two or three hundred cartmen, wearing aprons trimmed with blue, mounted.

25. A body of two hundred riflemen, dressed in frocks, plaid, leopard skin, and yellow, suitably trimmed.

26. A company of artillery, with two field pieces.

27. A brigade of about fifteen hundred infantrymen, in uniform.

28. The New Jersey cavalry.

29. A body of about three hundred farmers from the neighboring countryside.

48. Ribbon engraved "The Companion of Washington, The Nation's Guest." Portrait of Lafayette in sunburst. "Sold by H. Korn 82 N 2nd St. Phila." *De Witt Collection, University of Hartford*

49. Printed ribbon with portraits of Lafayette and Washington. "Sold by H. Korn 82 N 2nd St. Phila." *De Witt Collection, University of Hartford*

Although one might think that there would be no one left to watch such a parade the population of Philadelphia had been more than doubled by an influx of citizens from outlying towns and the streets were jammed with people. The parade passed through numerous triumphal arches to the main arch in front of the State House. The plan for this arch was taken from the arch erected in honor of Septimius Severus at Rome and its dimensions were forty-five feet in width by twelve feet in depth. It embraced a basement story of Doric design to the height of twenty-four feet above the ground. The abutments on each side were decorated with figures of Fame painted in basso-relievo. Fame's arms were extended and held civic wreaths over the keystone of the arch. The wings on each side of the center arch, of the Ionic order, were decorated with niches and statues representing Liberty, Victory, Independence, and Plenty, each having appropriate mottos inscribed in corresponding panels. The whole of the edifice was surmounted by an entablature thirty feet from the pavement, which supported a flight of steps in the center, where the arms of the city was placed. On either side were figures of Justice and Liberty. The arch was designed by William Strickland and was erected under the direction of the Messrs. Warren, Darley, and Jefferson of the Chestnut Street Theatre.

The magnificent arch, simpler and more classic in design than would seem, was reproduced on a souvenir item shortly after the event. A silk handkerchief was printed by the Germantown Print Works to commemorate the spectacular reception. The top scene shows an engraving of the march into the city and the great arch erected in front of Independence Hall. The scene at the bottom of the handkerchief is "The Arrival of Genl. Lafayette at the Port of New York in the ship, *Cadmus,* Capt. Allyn, Aug. 17th, 1824." The textile is known to have been printed in sepia or in blue on white.

No contemporary print, however, can recall the excitement Philadelphia's citizens must have felt on seeing the enormous procession. The route of the parade was down Fourth Street to Elev-

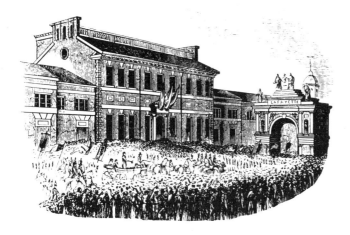

50. Triumphal arch built in Philadelphia in honor of Lafayette's visit to that city. *From an old engraving*

51. Silk handkerchief printed in Germantown, Pennsylvania, to commemorate Lafayette's visit to Philadelphia in 1824. Design was printed in blue or sepia. *Private collection*

enth Street to Chestnut Street to Eighth Street to Second Street. As Lafayette arrived at the State House (now Independence Hall) the U.S. frigate *John Adams,* anchored in the Delaware River opposite Chestnut Street, fired a salute. Mayor Joseph Watson escorted Lafayette inside the hall, where he read an address of welcome. Lafayette is said to have remarked at the time that he scarcely recognized the interior of the hall, which had been "modernized" several years previous to his visit. The remark was responsible for a restoration to its original appearance in 1828.

The speeches started at five in the afternoon and, despite the late hour, Lafayette remained in the hall as thousands of citizens filed by to shake his hand. Mechanics, magistrates, farmers, soldiers, sailors, and children were all admitted in the line of townspeople that filed past for several hours.

After this, Lafayette was escorted to the Mansion House on Third Street, which was his quarters while a guest of the citizens of Philadelphia. During the evening he found time to visit the wife of Robert Morris and to go to a banquet at Washington Hall that was attended by all the public officials. As usual, numerous toasts were drunk, including one "to Greece regenerated, wishing her a Washington for a leader, and a Lafayette for a friend."

That same evening at about quarter past six a spectacular general illumination on the streets of Philadelphia took place. It lasted three-quarters of an hour and attracted most of the population of the city back into the streets. The triumphal arches shone with hundreds of small lamps. Public buildings, such as the university, the Masonic Hall, the theater, the customhouse, and even coffee houses, were all adorned with elegant transparencies. The Bank of the United States was lighted by hundreds of small lamps hidden behind its columns and resembled, according to one witness, "those alabaster palaces which are described in fairy tales." Transparencies had been installed in the windows of private houses as well and the subjects of these were generally the "Nation's Guest" and "Washington." Flowers and lamps or candlesticks were used

52. March "La Fayette's Welcome" was written in advance of Lafayette's visit to Philadelphia and commissioned by Philadelphia Committee of Arrangement. *Courtesy American Antiquarian Society*

in many windows and the entire city shone in this magnificent display.

It has been estimated that one hundred and sixty thousand people walked about and gazed at the wonderous illumination, and while the city of Philadelphia glowed there was complete orderliness among the crowds in the streets. On the following morning the mayor, Joseph Watson, remarked to Lafayette, "See how freemen behave! More than forty thousand strangers have come to participate in the rejoicings of my fellow citizens, and I have not found it necessary to increase the number of watchmen. We have but a hundred and sixty, who are unarmed, and they have not had a single tumult to repress in this night of joyous and popular effervescence! Examine these reports! Not a single complaint—not the slightest trouble." Evidently, law and order were less of a problem in 1824 than they are one hundred and fifty years later.

September 29 was declared "Lafayette Day" in Philadelphia and it started with a reception in the old State House. Officers of the Municipal Corporation entertained the guest of honor at a dinner in the evening and on the next day Lafayette's time was filled with a reception for the Committee of the Philosophical Society, the Bar, the French citizens of Philadelphia, and other groups. A concert in Masonic Hall was held that night.

On the first of October Lafayette held a reception for other civic committees and had dinner with Governor Shulze. It is also reported that he took time to call on Hannah Till, a black woman who had been cook to him and George Washington. She was then living at 182 South Fourth Street and it is said that when Lafayette found that her house was mortgaged he arranged to have the debt cancelled. On the same day he also attended a reception at the home of Nicholas Biddle at 273 Chestnut Street. On the following day he visited the Navy Yard, where a banquet was spread in his honor in the old loft.

The next day, Sunday, was relatively quiet. Lafayette went to church services at Christ Church in the morning and in the afternoon attended vespers at St. Augustine's Roman Catholic Church. In the evening he was a guest of Judge Richard Peters.

The grandest celebration of Philadelphia's citizens was yet to be held. On October 4 Lafayette addressed about three thousand school children on State House Lawn, now Independence Square, dined with Revolutionary officers at the Mansion House, and then prepared to be guest of honor at a ball reported to be grander than any social function previously held in the city of Philadelphia. The new Chestnut Street Theatre was the site of the great Lafayette civic ball.

The entire floor of the theater had been painted for the occasion from designs furnished by the artist Strickland, but only those who arrived very early ever got to see it. The lobby was converted into a magnificent saloon, adorned with rose, orange, and lemon trees in full bloom and a profusion of green shrubbery. Pictures, busts, and banners with classical inscriptions of a patriotic nature were illuminated with hundreds of small lamps.

The house and the stage were decorated for dancing. The upper part of the house was hung with scarlet drapery studded with gold stars, and two additional chandeliers were hung alongside the great chandelier. A row of wax tapers was arranged over the canopy and the first and second tiers of boxes were crowded with the ladies of Philadelphia dressed in their finest ball gowns. The stage was decorated in the manner of an Eastern pavilion in a garden and terminated with the view of an extended sea and landscape lighted by the setting sun. Curiously, this scene was meant to typify the Western world. A multitude of chandeliers further lighted the stage area.

Twenty-two hundred tickets to the ball had been issued and at least six or seven hundred of these were allocated to "invited strangers" or people who lived outside the city limits. When Lafayette appeared at nine o'clock the women formed an avenue to the bottom of the stage through which he was escorted and, upon reaching the end, was greeted by the governor and mayor. The band played special marches written for the ball and as soon as the speeches were over the dancers were called and the revelry did not cease until five o'clock in the morning. Among the illustrious guests attending was the Secretary of State, John Quincy Adams.

Numerous other celebrations were held that week and Lafayette was a guest of many of the leading associations and citizens of the city. It was a busy week and more gifts were presented to the hero, among them a box made from the wood of the tree under which William Penn had made his treaty with the Indians. In all, Levasseur, George, and General Lafayette spent eight busy days inspecting all the wonders of Philadelphia, and at eight o'clock on Tuesday, October 5, they left the city by boat for Chester, whose citizens greeted them and joined them in yet another parade and banquet.

10

RECEPTIONS AT BALTIMORE AND WASHINGTON

The town of Chester was, as everywhere else Lafayette entered after dusk, brilliantly illuminated. If the tour was good for American business, the candlemakers must have been those who profited most. As a sentimental gesture the General was received in the same hall in which his wounds had been dressed after he had received them in the battle of Brandywine. Supper, prepared and served by the the women of the town, was the major entertainment.

The next morning Lafayette and his Pennsylvania escort left for Wilmington, Delaware. When the group reached the border of the state the Pennsylvania escort returned home and the Delaware Committee joined the travelers. After a brief visit to the battlefield of Brandywine, a reception was held in the Wilmington town hall, where most of the population of six thousand had a chance to see the hero.

Lafayette's next destination was a private commitment and he left at five o'clock in order to get to New Castle, where he had promised to be present at the wedding of Charles I. Du Pont to Dorcas Van Dyke. He did not arrive at Frenchtown, Maryland, until two in the morning, when he embarked on the steamboat *United States* for his entry into Baltimore.

A short distance from Frenchtown a deputation from Maryland joined Lafayette aboard the boat and they informed him that he was to be taken to Fort McHenry, where the governor of Maryland was prepared to receive him. Also aboard was John Quincy Adams.

Sleeping arrangements on board were somewhat crowded and Lafayette, George, and Levasseur were assigned to a single cabin. Others, including Adams, were bedded down wherever they could find room. When George Lafayette learned that Adams was being treated equally with guests of lesser stature he begged Adams to take his bed, but the Secretary of State refused, saying that he was very well accommodated and would be aggrieved to separate the father from his son. Levasseur then arrived on deck and, viewing the crowded and uncomfortable conditions, offered Adams his bed. Adams again refused, giving as an excuse that it would be an insult to the Committee on Arrangements if their plans were upset. The problem was finally solved when the committee members were consulted and another bed for Adams was moved into Lafayette's cabin. "If there be any aristocracy in American manners," wrote Levasseur of the incident, "it must at least be confessed that the great officers of the government partake of no such privileges."

"Exceeding bad weather" made it difficult to sleep that night but in the morning the sun shone as the boat steamed through the Patapsco River toward Fort McHenry and Baltimore. At nine o'clock four steamboats, the *Maryland,* the *Virginia,* the *Philadelphia,* and the *Eagle,* all decorated with flags and streamers and crowded with a multitude of citizens, escorted the *United States* toward shore. A number of smaller boats joined the others and Lafayette and other notables were rowed to shore in a boat that had Captain Gardner of the *United States* and Baltimore shipmasters as coxswain and crew.

At the gate of Fort McHenry Lafayette was surrounded by veterans of the War of 1812 and it was clear that many of them had been mutilated. The damaged flag from that war was again raised as Lafayette entered the fort and the roar of cannon announced to the citizens of Baltimore that Lafayette had arrived. A detachment of infantry, magistrates, and old Revolutionary soldiers stood on parade and by opening their ranks revealed to Lafayette the tent of Washington. A sentimental moment occurred as Lafayette and his son met with Washington's nephew, Mr. Custis. Tears and embraces were in order as Lafayette remembered his past association with Washington and George recalled the months he had spent with the Washington family, as a youth.

Lafayette was received under the tent by Governor Stevens and speeches were exchanged. The General inspected the garrison at the fort and then led the procession into Baltimore in an open carriage drawn by four white horses. The carriage passed through lines of militia on the left, which fell into the procession once they had been passed. On the right were the crowds of citizens of Baltimore and surrounding towns. Under the triumphal arch, erected at the entrance to the city, were twenty-four young ladies dressed in white and crowned with wreaths of myrtle. Each bore a lance upon which was inscribed a name of each of the states of the Union. They encircled Lafayette and crowned him with wreaths and the procession continued to the front of City Hall.

After the welcoming speeches and introductions to the members of the city council Lafayette was led to an alcove built in the center of the city. It was draped with rich carpets. While the band of the militia of Maryland favored the crowds with a rendition of "Lafayette's March" and other music specially written for the occasion, the General reviewed the troops and was then taken to the Fountain Inn on Light Street, where headquarters for him had been established.

The busy first day in Baltimore included a dinner attended by representatives of the governments of the city and state. John Quincy Adams offered a toast in which he described the scene at Washington's tent that morning: "The tears of glory, gratitude, and joy, shed under the tent of Washington." At the great ball held in the evening the theater was illuminated with gaslight as Lafayette entered.

In all, Lafayette spent five days in Baltimore and would return to the city several times during the remainder of the year. On this official welcome, however, he was honored by all the usual civic

53. Lafayette ribbon made for his reception in Baltimore has scene of Cornwallis resigning his sword at Yorktown. Marked "Sold at J. Goulds Military Warehouse, Baltimore." *De Witt Collection, University of Hartford*

54. "Genl. La Fayette's Waltz," written in honor of the visit to Baltimore in September 1824. *Courtesy American Antiquarian Society*

55. The Capitol at Washington in 1824. *From an old engraving*

and fraternal groups and visited all the public institutions of the city. A degree was conferred upon him by the University of Maryland and he also visited Peale's Museum.

By this time it had been observed that Lafayette displayed a strength that was almost supernatural and he seemed to thrive on the adulation he received. On the evening before his departure from Baltimore, the General, George, and Auguste visited General Smith and decided to walk the short distance to their hotel. Although they had hoped to pass through the streets unnoticed, "the size and gait of General Lafayette betrayed us," wrote Levasseur. A great crowd gathered around and George Lafayette felt himself being pulled by the coattails. When he turned around he saw a beautiful young girl, who said to him in a touching voice, "I beseech you to enable me but to touch him and you will make me happy." General Lafayette, upon hearing her, turned and gave her his hand which she seized and kissed. This happening was not unusual and it seemed to be the aim of thousands of Americans to say they had touched or been touched by Lafayette.

Although only forty-five years before Baltimore had been a small collection of "badly built houses," it was, in 1824, one of the most beautiful cities in the country. Its inhabitants were prosperous and Levasseur noted that "they did not neglect to enlarge their taste for the intellect." Lafayette expressed his hope that the four thousand slaves in the city would soon be freed.

On the day before he left Baltimore for Washington, Lafayette wrote a letter to his family at La Grange:

Here we are at Baltimore; we have been received under the most touching circumstances; we all wept, embracing old comrades under General Washington's tent—the ministers of different denominations paid me a visit: the good Quakers told me that religious scruples had prevented them from signing an address in which military success was referred to —All the pleasures of my journey will not prevent my enjoying, more than ever, that of going back to the farm at La Grange to see my dear daughters and my dear sons. You can guess that at these brilliant fêtes and charming balls, I always regret not to be able to bring my grand-daughters to them.

On Sunday, October 10, Lafayette's final day on this visit to Baltimore, he attended high mass at the Roman Catholic cathedral. "Sunday," wrote Levasseur, "is a rather dull day; religious observances are austere, though the most perfect liberty of conscience exists."

Lafayette's departure from Baltimore was as brilliant as his entry. Troops paraded on the plain between the city and Fort McHenry, after which a farewell dinner was held under an immense tent. There were, of course, many toasts, not only to Lafayette, but to the officers attending who had distinguished themselves during the War of 1812. The emotional high point of the afternoon was a rendition by a young officer of a song written especially for the General. When it came time for the young man to pronounce the hero's name, he went to pieces, could not finish, and fell sobbing on Lafayette's hand.

At four in the afternoon the party ended and the travelers left to enter their waiting carriages. While Lafayette and his son were literally carried in triumph upon the shoulders of the citizens of Baltimore, Levasseur got lost in the shuffle and had to manage as best he could to keep up with them. After such a tiring day the march out of the city was cut short, and Lafayette, wanting to enter Washington by daylight, spent the night in Rossburg.

Accompanied by Governor Sprigg of Maryland, Lafayette left Rossburg at nine o'clock on Tuesday, October 8, for his entry into Washington. He was met outside of the city by officials, volunteer cavalry, other troops, and private citizens. At the city line he was transferred to an open barouche and the procession continued to the Capitol. An arch of triumph through which Lafayette passed had been erected in his honor and welcoming ceremonies were held on the steps of the Capitol building.

The procession then moved slowly through throngs of school-children, militia, and private citizens to the White House. The gates to the grounds were not guarded, but when the crowds accompanying the procession reached the fence they stopped and only the city authorities accompanied Lafayette into the President's house. Levasseur's impressions of the moment when he entered the White House for the first time are of interest:

A single domestic opened the principal door, and we were immediately introduced into the hall of audience, which is of considerable size, elliptical in shape, and decorated and carpeted with a remarkable correctness of taste. The President at the upper end of the room, was seated upon a chair not differing in form or elevation from the rest, and had near him the four secretaries of the cabinet, the officers of the army and navy; some senators and public officers were arranged in a semicircle on his right and left. Like the President, they were all dressed in plain blue, without lace, embroidery or decorations, without any of those puerile ornaments for which so many silly men dance attendance in the antichambers of European palaces.

When Lafayette came into the room the entire assembly rose to greet him and President Monroe came forward and embraced him. He also shook hands with George and Auguste and introduced them to the entire company. Monroe's welcoming address was short and hospitable:

You are aware from my last letter how much I desired to have you in my house along with your two companions, during your stay in this city; but I am obliged to renounce this pleasure. The people of Washington claim you; they say that as the Nation's Guest, none but the nation has a right to lodge you. I must yield to the public will, and the municipality have prepared a hotel, provided a carriage, and in short, anticipated all your wants. You must accept their invitation, but I hope that this will not hinder you from considering my house as your own. You will always find your places ready at my table, and I wish whenever you have no engagements with citizens that you will dine with me. This evening, the municipality expect you at a public banquet: tomorrow you will be present at a grand dinner which I give to the principal officers of government, but once these ceremonies are concluded, I will do everything I can, that you may be as frequently as possible, a part of my family.

Following the President's reception Lafayette was escorted to the Franklin Hotel, on Pennsylvania Avenue and Nineteenth Street. Innkeeper Gadsby was host to the Lafayette party. In spite of the public banquet that evening Lafayette found time to visit Martha Custis in her home in Georgetown and during his long stay in Washington spent as much time as posible with all members of the Washington family.

The following morning Lafayette had breakfast with President Monroe at the White House and during the day he visited Columbia College. At the State dinner in the evening he, George, and Auguste were introduced to Mrs. Monroe, her two daughters, and her sons-in-law. Levasseur's observation that "Mrs. Monroe is a fine and very agreeable woman" might not have been shared by Washington society. The secretary, accustomed to the implied power of European thrones, was impressed with the democratic simplicity of the dinner and remarked that the only chair that was distinguished from all the rest was for Lafayette, the guest of honor.

The next day Lafayette paid a visit to the Jesuit College, at Georgetown, where he was welcomed by Superior Monsigneur Legendre. He took his noon meal with Martha Custis and had an informal dinner at the White House. The following day he breakfasted with Secretary of the Navy Crawford and visited the Navy Yard. While his employer visited with many old friends during this week Levasseur had time to wander around Washington and to examine its public buildings. "The plan of Washington is so gigantic that it will require a century for its completion," he prophesied.

On Saturday Lafayette once again went to the Navy Yard where a procession for his entry into Alexandria was formed. A reception and banquet were held in that town in his honor and following these he returned to Washington.

11

A SENTIMENTAL JOURNEY

Lafayette's presence was required at the celebration of the anniversary of the capture of Yorktown and he departed Washington on the sixteenth of October and crossed the Potomac to the thunder of artillery. That night John Quincy Adams informed the hero of the death of Louis XVIII, King of France. The following morning Lafayette boarded the steamboat *Petersburg* and after a voyage downriver of two hours the guns of Fort Washington announced that the party, which included Mr. Calhoun, the Secretary of War, several generals, and private citizens, was approaching Mount Vernon. A military band, also aboard, struck up suitably plaintive music as Lafayette came on deck. Levasseur reported that at the sight of the last home of Washington, "an involuntary and spontaneous movement made us kneel."

Small boats landed the party at Mount Vernon and a carriage took Lafayette along the path to the house where he was met by three nephews of Washington and conducted to the tomb of the first President of the United States. This was the most solemn and touching moment of a year filled with nostalgia and sentiment and the subject inspired many artistic renditions of the scene for years following the event. The subject of death as a heroic event had not yet reached the zenith it would in the later nineteenth century, but printed scenes of "Lafayette at the Tomb of Washington" decorated plates, platters, and jugs with which the Staffordshire potters flooded the American market.

At the moment that Lafayette entered the simple tomb cannons thundered from the fort. Lafayette descended alone into the vault and reappeared a few moments later, his eyes swimming with tears. He then took his son and Levasseur and led them into the tomb. He wordlessly pointed to the coffin, threw a kiss to the remains of George Washington, and all three fell sobbing into each other's arms. When the three emerged from the tomb Washington's nephews presented Lafayette with a gold ring containing a lock of their uncle's hair and the somber group returned to the house, which was then occupied by one of the nephews, a judge of the Supreme Court, who bore his uncle's name.

Each of the visiting triumvirate had cut a cypress branch from the site of Washington's tomb and these were carried on the solemn march back to the steamboat. "We resembled," wrote Levasseur, "a bereaved family, who had entombed a beloved father, recently dead." The silence was not broken as the party boarded the *Petersburg,* but after Mount Vernon had faded from sight everyone gathered on the quarter-deck to listen to Lafayette relate stories of his old friend.

Shortly after leaving Mount Vernon the *Petersburg* was joined by the steamboat *Potomac,* which was carrying a volunteer company from Fredericksburg and a great number of passengers who had come to escort General Lafayette to Yorktown. The two boats exchanged salutes and sailed in tandem through the night, arriving at the mouth of the York River at noon on Monday, the eighteenth. Five more boats joined these two and the small fleet entered the river to travel together to Yorktown. Lafayette was met by the Yorktown Committee, the governor of Virginia, Chief Justice John Marshall, many officers of the Army, and crowds of people, many of whom had traveled great distances for the occasion. His headquarters was the house that Cornwallis had inhabited during the siege of Yorktown forty-three years before.

Yorktown had not been rebuilt since the famous battle. The houses were still in ruins, blackened by fire or pierced by bullets. The ground was covered with fragments of arms, broken shells, and overturned gun-carriages. Tents were grouped or scattered according to the nature of the terrain and small platoons of soldiers placed at various points were purposely meant to convey the idea of a camp hastily formed near a village taken and occupied after a fierce battle. This scene had been contrived for Lafayette's benefit and since show business seemed to take precedence over comfort, only Lafayette was given a bed. The remainder of the party, including George and Auguste, was given straw pallets to spread out anywhere. A volunteer company of sixty officers guarded the sleeping hero throughout the night.

At daybreak cannon thundered throughout the area, calling all the surrounding troops to arms. Lafayette, accompanied by the Committee of Arrangement, went to Washington's tent, which had been brought by boat from Fort McHenry, to receive the various corps of officers from the surrounding regiments. Two old Revolutionary officers were reported to have fainted upon shaking hands with him.

At eleven o'clock the troops formed two columns and conducted the General through a triumphal arch, where he was received by General Taylor, who spoke eloquently of Lafayette's many virtues. Lafayette replied with words of praise for the other officers who had directed the attack at Yorktown and accepted a wreath in their honor.

On the same day, some servants, while searching through the house that had sheltered Cornwallis, found a large chest in the corner of the cellar that had been there since the siege. Upon examination the box was found to contain a supply of candles and these were placed in a circle in the center of the camp, where they were lighted to define the area where dancing took place that evening. Since the dancing didn't stop until the candles were entirely consumed no one got any sleep. By dawn the troops departed, a military breakfast was held on the battlefield for the guests, and at two in the afternoon Lafayette left Yorktown for a trip to Williamsburg. Governor Pleasants and an escort accompanied him.

In 1824 Williamsburg was already in need of restoration. The former capital of Virginia was described by Levasseur as "a small town, . . . at present retaining very little of its ancient importance." He bemoaned the fact that its college, founded under the reign of William and Mary and celebrated for the excellence of its learning until less than half a century before, had since appeared to have partaken the sad destiny of the town. Lafayette inspected the college and attended a banquet given him by the town's five hundred citizens, who also held a ball as the final celebration.

The following morning, October 22, the group left Williamsburg for Jamestown, where they once more boarded the *Petersburg*. On steaming down the James River toward Norfolk Lafayette reminisced with some of his old friends on their Virginia campaign during the Revolution. At his landing General Lafayette was saluted by the two forts that defended the entrance to the river and by the many boats that had gathered in the port.

Although the festivities at Norfolk included the usual reception, civic ceremonies, and banquets, Levasseur, in his account of the trip, did not go into detail about any of these celebrations. He was not impressed by the city and said, "Of all the cities we visited, Norfolk had the least agreeable aspect. The houses are generally badly built and the streets narrow and crooked. On account of the adjacent marshes the air is unhealthy and diseases common during the autumn." Both he and his illustrious employer were strongly against slavery and it must have been an embarrassment for them that the many French settlers of the town, emigrants from St. Domingo, hired out to hard labor slaves they had brought with them. The slaves worked in the harbor, were badly fed, and were forced to turn over their meager wages to their French owners.

On Monday the party left Norfolk for Richmond and after visiting the Portsmouth Navy Yard and inspecting a new sixty-four-gun ship, the *North Carolina*, reentered Norfolk to be entertained by the Freemasons. Lafayette left the ball given in his honor that night around eleven o'clock and boarded the *Petersburg* for a trip

56. *Left* Washington's tomb as it appeared during Lafayette's visit to Mount Vernon. From painting by William Mathew Prior (1806–73). Prior painted same view many times, this one *circa* 1846. *Courtesy Old Sturbridge Village.*

57. *Right* Ticket to ball given in Lafayette's honor at Yorktown on October 19, 1824. Of special importance, since there seems to be no other record of the event having taken place or of Lafayette having attended. *Courtsy American Antiquarian Society*

58. Monticello, home of Thomas Jefferson in 1825. *From an old woodcut*

to Richmond. This city was impatient to receive Lafayette and claimed the largest proportion among its citizenry of former companions-in-arms of the General.

Lafayette's entry into Richmond had to be delayed because of heavy rains and did not take place until the following morning. When the receptions finally did start Lafayette received about forty Revolutionary soldiers who had served under him in Virginia and this emotional moment was heightened by the General calling many of these old men by name. The major welcoming address was given by John Marshall and on the second evening of his Richmond visit Lafayette attended theatrical performances given in his honor. He also attended horse races the next day and the name of a winning mare was changed from "Jeanette" to "Virginia Lafayette." A ball ended the day.

The following day Lafayette left Richmond for Petersburg. His original plan had been to go straight from Richmond to the home of his old friend Thomas Jefferson, but representatives from towns along or near his proposed route pressed invitations upon him. The overland route to Petersburg through woods and over sandy roads took six hours and during the reception, banquet, and ball the citizens of the town delighted in pointing out how much the town had benefited from Lafayette having ordered it burned during the Revolution. "At that time," he was told, "we had none but miserable wooden houses to receive you in, and now there are large well built brick dwellings in which we can offer you all the comforts of life."

Because of a luncheon and many requests for him to address the schoolchildren, Lafayette was not able to leave for Richmond until two in the afternoon the next day. He was due at a reception to be given by Richmond's Masonic fraternity that evening. This particular entertainment was one of the few examples of poor planning during the year's tour. First, the three, Auguste, George, and Lafayette, were inducted into the orders at the Masonic Temple, which was at one end of the town. They then were conducted in a grand procession to a fraternal banquet at the hotel situated at the other end of the town and after the dinner and many toasts the procession was repeated in reverse back to the Masonic Hall. After this, Lafayette, George, and Auguste were obliged to make the long trip back across the city once again to their quarters at the Eagle Hotel.

The next day was Sunday and except for attendance at church services in the morning and a dinner party at the hotel it was otherwise quiet. On Monday John Marshall entertained the trio at his home and on Tuesday, November 2, Lafayette left Richmond for the first stop, the village of Goochland Court House, of what would be a difficult eighty-mile journey. He went through Columbia and Wilmington, where he spent a night, but was anxious to see Jefferson, to talk over old times, and to visit Monticello. Although Lafayette appeared to be as robust as ever, the pace finally caught up with his secretary, and the day Lafayette was to reach Monticello, Levasseur awoke too weak to move. George stayed behind to comfort him and the two arrived at Jefferson's home after Lafayette.

The procession to Monticello had been slow. Stops were made in towns of Fluvana and Albemarle counties and Lafayette was obliged to attend all the entertainments the citizens had prepared for him. His eventual meeting with Jefferson was described as "tearful" and the *Central Gazette* of Albemarle reported that the two old friends "embraced again and again."

Thomas Jefferson was well known for his hospitality and his reception of Lafayette was lavish. His home always had been open to visitors and the enormous plantation, the house, and its furnishings left a strong impression on Levasseur. Although he admitted to the seeming well-being of Jefferson's slaves, he deplored their existence in a democracy and thought that Monticello would have been more profitable if Jefferson had run it with paid, rather than slave, labor.

Thomas Jefferson accompanied Lafayette on a short visit the

next morning to Charlottesville, where a reception at the University of Virginia had been planned. There they were met by James Madison, and Levasseur noted, "The sight of the Nation's Guest, seated at the patriotic banquet between Jefferson and Madison, excited in those present an enthusiasm which expressed itself in enlivening sallies of wit and humour." Madison's toast, "To Liberty, with virtue for her guest and gratitude for the feast," was, according to reports, received with "transports of applause."

A tour of the university, where George Washington Lafayette was presented with a strange gift, a live American rattlesnake, terminated with a return of Lafayette, Madison, and Jefferson to Monticello. It was time for a well-deserved rest and Lafayette remained a guest of Jefferson for nine more days during which he and Levasseur caught up on some of the voluminous correspondence that had reached them. The mail from Europe alone amounted to some six hundred letters and there was even more mail from Americans, much of which required immediate answers. In the evenings the guests held long conversations with their host and his neighboring planters and the matter of slavery was discussed at length, with Madison and Jefferson and the neighbors taking an opposite viewpoint from Lafayette's.

A deputation from the town of Fredericksburg, Virginia, arrived at Monticello on Tuesday, November 9, to invite Lafayette to visit and on the fifteenth Lafayette and Madison said goodbye to Jefferson and left for Montpelier. On the nineteenth an escort called for Lafayette and he went to Fredericksburg, stopping on the way at Orange Court House, where, after welcoming ceremonies, James Madison left and rode back to his own estate.

Lafayette was met at Wilderness Tavern, outside of Fredericksburg, by the Committee of Arrangements and escorted in a parade into the town, where a reception was held. The General and his traveling companions probably would have been less than happy had they read this notice in the *Virginia Herald:* "Owners of slaves are respectfully solicited to keep their slaves within their lots. All colored people are warned that they are not to appear on any of the streets through which the procession will pass."

The next day was Sunday and the town Masons escorted Lafayette to services at the Episcopal church and then held a reception for him. The next day, after a civic reception at Gray's Tavern the citizens and militia of Fredericksburg marched with Lafayette to the bank of the Potomac, where a boat waited to take the hero back to Washington.

12

REPUBLICANS ARE NOT ALWAYS UNGRATEFUL

Upon arriving in Washington Lafayette was taken to Gadsby's Hotel and that evening dined with President Monroe and the mayor of Washington. The following morning, Wednesday, November 24, a delegation of Choctaw Indian chiefs called on him and after lunch Lafayette set out with an escort for Baltimore to attend the annual meeting of the Agricultural Society of Maryland.

The meeting of the Agricultural Society was much like today's country fairs, with awards for excellence in livestock and crops. Horses, cows, hogs, and sheep were exhibited and models of newly developed farm implements were of extreme interest to Lafayette, "the farmer of La Grange." After a banquet and many toasts on the fairgrounds Lafayette was charged with handing out the awards for exhibits. Following this he was escorted into the city by the Lafayette Cadets and at the Baltimore Theater attended a performance of *School for Scandal,* a play with which he was well acquainted by this time.

During the next few days Lafayette visited several farms in the area and took notes on improvements that might be helpful to him at La Grange. He was given a young bull and two heifers of English Devonshire breed by a Mr. Patterson, and other Maryland breeders presented him with turkeys and hogs. These were all shipped to La Grange.

On Friday evening Lafayette was present at a performance of *The Bride of Abydos* and the next day went to the cattle show and had dinner with the president of the Agricultural Society. He was escorted back to Washington on Monday morning and that evening saw a performance of *She Stoops to Conquer* at the Washington Theatre.

By this time Washington was bustling with activity. Congress was about to reconvene, ambassadors from Europe and South America had returned to their posts, and Indian deputations had arrived to deal with the federal government. Waiting for Lafayette in Washington were invitations from all the southern and western states which begged for his presence. In addition, congressional representatives called on him in large numbers to apprise him of the elaborate preparations that were being made in their home states and to ask for a firm commitment.

Plans were made to accept as many of the invitations as possible. Lafayette would appear in every one of the twenty-four states, but this part of the journey would not take place until spring, partly because of the weather and the condition of the roads in the less populated areas and partly because he wanted to attend the sessions of Congress. In the meantime, he visited as much as possible with members of the Washington family.

On Saturday, December 4, Lafayette, George, and Auguste attended a gala performance at the Washington Theatre, where Mrs. Dinneford appeared in *The Soldier's Daughter*. The next day, although he knew Congress would reconvene, Lafayette went to Woodlawn, the estate of Washington's niece, Mrs. Lewis. As Lafayette had been informed, President Monroe planned to ask, in his opening address to Congress, that the people of the United States make some monetary award to Lafayette. The next day the representative of Pennsylvania, Mr. Mitchell, made a motion that Lafayette be invited to take a seat within the rail when he attended sessions of the governing body.

An urgent order of business of Congress of 1824 was to appoint committees to arrange the ceremonial for the public reception of Lafayette by Congress upon his return to Washington on the eighth, the joint committees reported that each house of Congress should receive the hero separately. An invitation was brought to Lafayette to attend a session of the Senate on Friday of that week, but for some reason the ceremony took place the day before.

It became known to Lafayette that the national troops wished to parade during the congressional reception, but at his request the idea was abandoned. He felt it was inconsistent with his character and situation to appear before Congress with the "pomp of arms" and at half past noon on December 9 a committee of the Senate called on Lafayette in carriages and accompanied him and his two traveling companions to the Capitol. At precisely one o'clock the doors of the Senate chamber were opened and General Lafayette was led into the hall by Mr. Barbour, chairman of the Senate committee. Upon arriving at the center of the hall Mr. Barbour announced, "We introduce General Lafayette to the Senate of the United States." This simple announcement was received with a "profound silence," followed by a motion to adjourn. The Senators then successively left their seats to shake hands with Lafayette and welcome him individually.

The following morning Lafayette was again conducted to the Capitol, this time by a deputation of twenty-four members of the House of Representatives. The procession, devoid of pomp or circumstance, consisted of a dozen carriages. Upon arrival, the nation's guest was led to a committee room while the galleries filled to capacity and the members took their seats. A proposal was made that the Senate should be invited to attend the session and members of the House moved to the right to make room. Two members of Congress escorted George Washington Lafayette and Auguste Levasseur to honored seats and a signal was then given whereby General Lafayette, escorted by members of the committee, walked into the room. At his entrance the entire body rose and removed their hats in silence. The major address was given by Henry Clay:

General—The house of representatives of the United States, impelled alike by its own feelings, and by those of the whole American people, could not have assigned to me a more gratifying duty, than that of presenting to you cordial congratulations upon the occasion of your recent arrival in the United States, in compliance with the wishes of congress, and to assure you of the very high satisfaction which your presence affords on this early theatre of your glory and reknown. Although but few members who compose this body shared with you in the war of our revolution all have, from impartial history or from faithful tradition, a knowledge of the perils, the sufferings, and the sacrifices which you voluntarily encountered, and the signal services, in America and Europe, which you performed for an infant, a distant, and an alien people; and all feel and own the very great extent of the obligations under which you have placed our country. But the relations in which you have ever stood to the United States, interesting and important as they have been, do not constitute the only motive of the respect and admiration which the house of representatives entertain for you. Your consistency of character, your uniform devotion to regulated liberty, in all the vicissitudes of a long and arduous life, also commands its admiration. During all the recent convulsions of Europe, amidst, as after the dispersion of, every political storm, the people of the United States have beheld you, true to your old principles, firm and erect, cheering and animating, with your well known voice, the voteries of liberty, its faithful and fearless champion, ready to shed that last drop of blood which here you so freely and nobly spilt, in the same holy cause.

The vain wish has been sometimes indulged, that Providence would allow the patriot, after death, to return to his country, and to contemplate the intermediate changes which had taken place—to view the forests felled, the cities built, the mountains levelled, the canals cut, the highways constructed, the progress of the arts, the advancement of learning and the increase in population—General, your present visit to the United States is a realization of the consoling object of that wish. You are in the midst of posterity. Every where, you must have been struck with the great changes, physical and moral, which have occurred since you left us. Even this city, bearing a venerated name, alike endeared to you and to us, has since emerged from the forest which then covered its site. In one respect, you behold us unaltered, and this is in the sentiment of continued devotion to liberty, and of ardent affection and profound gratitude to your departed friend, the father of his country, and to you, and to your illustrious associates in the field and in the cabinet, for the multiplied blessings which surround us, and for the very privilege of addressing you, which I now exercise. This sentiment, now fondly cherished by more than ten millions of people, will be transmitted, with unabated vigour, down the tide of time, through the countless millions of people, who are destined to inhabit this continent, to the latest posterity.

Everyone in the audience waited "with profound emotion" for Lafayette to read a prepared speech. Instead he took a few steps forward, and after a few moments when he seemed to be collecting his thoughts, delivered an extemporaneous answer no less moving than Clay's address:

My obligations to the United States, sir, far exceed any merit I might claim; they date from the time when I have had the happiness to be adopted as a young soldier, a favored son of America; they have been continued to me during almost a half a century of constant affection and confidence; and now, sir, thanks to your most gratifying invitation, I find myself greeted by a series of welcomes, one hour of which would more than compensate for the public exertions and sufferings of a whole life.

The approbation of the American people, and their representatives, for my conduct, during the vicissitudes of the European revolution, is the highest reward I could receive. Well may I stand firm and erect, when, in their names, and by you, Mr. Speaker, I am declared to have, in every instance, been faithful to those American principles of liberty, equality, and true social order, the devotion to which, as it has been from my earliest youth, so it shall continue to be to my latest breath.

You have been pleased, Mr. Speaker, to allude to the peculiar felicity of my situation, when, after so long an absence, I am called to witness the immense improvements, the admirable communications, the prodigious creations, of which we find an example in this city, whose name itself is a venerated palladium; in a word, all the grandeur and prosperity of those happy United States, who, at the same time they nobly secure the complete assertion of American independence, reflect, on every part of the world, the light of a far superior political civilization.

What better pledge can be given, of a persevering national love of liberty, when these blessings are evidently the result of a virtuous resistance to oppression, and institutions founded on the rights of man, and the republican principle of self-government.

No, Mr. Speaker, posterity has not begun for me, since, in the sons of my companions and friends, I find the same public feelings in my behalf, which I have had the happiness to experience in their fathers.

Sir, I have been allowed, forty years ago, before a committee of congress of thirteen states, to express the fond wishes of an American heart; on this day, I have the honour and enjoy the delight, to congratulate the representatives of the Union, so vastly enlarged, on the realization of those wishes, even beyond human expectation, and upon the almost infinite prospects we can with certainty anticipate; permit me, Mr. Speaker and gentlemen of the house of representatives, to join to the expression of those sentiments, a tribute of my lively gratitude, affectionate devotion, and profound respect.

Lafayette's speech was widely acclaimed and both his and Clay's speeches were printed in many newspapers throughout the country. However, kind words were not all that Congress had in mind to show its appreciation for Lafayette's services. A committee was appointed to devise a way to present to Lafayette some sort of recompense or gift from the entire nation. Ideas offered in the press and mail to Congress showed that many people felt that the man who had spent most of his personal fortune in helping the nation establish its independence should be repaid with more than triumphal arches, banquets, and balls. By Sunday, December 12, it was known in Washington that Henry Clay had conferred with John Quincy Adams to discuss a grant of moncy for the General and that Clay opposed giving him a large amount.

It was no secret by now that Lafayette could use any money given him by Congress. Since his release from prison his debts had been mounting. La Grange was hardly a paying venture and the General had little talent for managing money. He once said, "I never stopped to count the dollars; and others may know, perhaps, as much about it as I do; but this I know, that whatever it was, it went freely and never for a moment regretted; but I gloried then, as I do now, that I have made so good a use of what fortune had been placed within my control. And as to my own services, whether great or small, I never taxed or received a dollar for them, either in the American or French Revolutions."

It could hardly have been a coincidence that Lafayette left the city on the sixteenth to go to Annapolis for a reception and celebration. He was still out of the city when, on December 20, a bill was reported out of committee that detailed the services rendered by Lafayette to America and listed the many sacrifices he had made in the cause of independence. The sum of two hundred thousand dollars and the fee simple of a tract of land of twenty-four thousand acres, to be chosen by the President from any lands that remained unsold, were voted to the General:

Be it enacted by the Senate and House of Representatives of the United States in Congress assembled, That the sum of two hundred thousand dollars be, and the same is hereby granted to Major General La Fayette, in compensation for his important services and expenditures during the American Revolution; and that for this purpose a stock to the amount be issued in his favour, dated the 4th of July, 1824, bearing an annual interest of six per cent., payable quarter yearly, and redeemable on the 31st of December, 1834.

And be it further enacted, That one complete Township of land be, and the same is hereby granted to the said Major General La Fayette; and that the President of the United States be authorized to cause said township to be located on any of the public lands which remain unsold; and that patents be issued to General La Fayette for the same.

The bill was made the order of the day in the Senate on the twenty-first, and although there was a little opposition to it (on the grounds that it would establish a precedent), Senator Hayne of South Carolina delivered a long speech explaining that a similar situation could never again arise, reiterating Lafayette's accomplishments and expenditures during the Revolution, and asking for a unanimous passage of the resolution. The bill passed, however, with some opposition—the vote was thirty-seven to seven— and on Monday, January 3, a presentation of the bill to Lafayette was read into the Record:

GENERAL: We are a Committee of the Senate and House of Representatives, charged with the office of informing you of the passage of an act, a copy of which we now present. You will perceive, from this act, Sir, that the two Houses of Congress, aware of the large pecuniary as well as other sacrifices which your long and arduous devotion to the cause of freedom has cost you, have deemed it their privilege to reimburse a portion of them as having been incurred in part on account of the United States. The principles which have marked your character will not permit you to oppose any objection to the discharge of so much of the national obligation to you as admits of it. We are directed to express to you the confidence as well as request of the two Houses of Congress, that you will, by an acquiescence in their wishes in this respect, add another to the many signal proofs you have offered of your esteem for a people whose esteem for you can never cease until they have ceased to prize the liberty they enjoy, and to venerate the virtues by which it was acquired. We have only to subjoin an expression of our gratification in being the organs of this communication, and of the distinguished personal respect with which we are, your obedient servants,

S. Smith	W. S. Archer
Robert Y. Hayne	S. Van Rensselaer
D. Bouligny	Philip S. Markley

Committee of the Senate, Committee of
the House of Representatives.
Washington, January 1, 1825

An answer was required to this message and Lafayette, who certainly must have been aware of President Monroe's message requesting the gift and the debates over it in the Senate, gave the following reply:

Gentlemen of the Committee of both Houses of Congress:
The immense and unexpected gift, which, in addition to former and considerable bounties, it had pleased Congress to confer upon me, calls for the warmest acknowledgements of an old American soldier, an adopted son of the United States, two titles dearer to my heart than all the treasure in the world.

However proud I am of every sort of obligation received from the people of the United States, and their Representatives in Congress the large extent of this benefaction might have created in my mind feeling of hesita-

THE
CARRIER'S ADDRESS

TO THE PATRONS OF THE

WASHINGTON WHIG.

JANUARY 1st, 1825.

'Tis quite the fashion now, each New-Year's morn,
  For News-boys to bear round their pithy rhymes,
All fill'd and bursting, like Orlando's horn,
  With sage ideas on the changing times,
To pour them on their Patrons—we, too, scorn,
  To let NEGLECT be number'd with our crimes;
For while these sports of fancy blaze around,
Some little spark in Bridgeton should be found.

We need not wake the ghosts of sages dead,
  Or call the spirits from the " vasty deep ; "
O'er nature's wild domains we need not tread,
  Or fly where sorrow's child makes stoick's weep,
To aid our *muse*, her tribute here to spread,
  Before our generous PATRONS———those who keep,
Their wits most wisely from the publick gaze,
May tell us what they would say—*should they please.*

Now gratitude wakes up her gentle fires,
  And LAFAYETTE receives a *just reward*;
Ye fashionable boasters who admire
  The liberal donors who this boon afford,
Say, was it *fame* to which they did aspire,
  By heaping cash upon the Hero's board?
But those who voted 'gainst the publick voice,
Consulted conscience also in their choice ?

Shame ! ye Divines—now SMYTH has beat you all !
  For the Apocalypse he has *unseal'd*;
He spied the *open'd door*, and in did crawl,
  And all the myst'ries were to him reveal'd;
The meaning of the HORNS, both *great* and *small*,
  And mystick TREE whose leaves the nations heal'd !
" 'Pon honour, " all these wonders he did see,
And who can doubt, for—Congressman is he.

59. In nineteenth-century newspapers printed "Carriers' Addresses," or poems relating the past year's events. Newsboys gave these to customers on the New Year. Almost all carriers' addresses for January 1, 1825, mention Lafayette's visit. This one, from *Washington Whig,* is of special interest, since it mentions reluctance of a few Congressmen to vote for gift to Lafayette. A huge party was held in Lafayette's honor on New Year's Day, 1825, in Washington. *Courtesy American Antiquarian Society*

tion, not inconsistent, I hope, with those of the most grateful reverence. But the so very kind resolutions of both Houses, delivered by you, gentlemen, in terms of equal kindness, precludes all other sentiments except those of the lively and profound gratitude of which, in respectfully accepting the munificent favor, I have the honour to beg you will be the organs.

Permit me also, gentlemen to join a tender of my affectionate personal thanks to the expression of the highest respect, with which I have the honour to be, your obedient servant,

Lafayette

Eyewitnesses to the presentation ceremony reported that Lafayette was "greatly embarrassed by this munificence" and at first seemed tempted to refuse it. Public opinion of the gift of the nation could not have been more approving and when word spread throughout the states by means of newspapers and broadsides the only attacks seemed to come from writers who were unhappy that a few members of Congress had voted against it. Some states, in order to compensate for what they felt was an insult to the greatness of Lafayette, attempted to create their own funds or land gifts for him, but Lafayette quashed all of these efforts.

It was said that when a member of Congress attempted to apologize to Lafayette for the opposition to the bill the General interrupted him by saying, "I, Sir, am one of the opposition. The gift is so munificent, so far exceeding the services of the individual, that had I been a member of Congress, I must have voted against it." This was widely quoted in the press and only added to Lafayette's immense popularity.

The "township" given to Lafayette and chosen by James Monroe was a section of Tallahassee, Florida, incorporated as a city in 1825. Contrary to the wishes of Congress, the gift did not keep Lafayette in America nor did it attract any of his descendants. The following letter from Lafayette to William P. Duval, dated February 28, 1827, shows that at that time the property was still in Lafayette's possession:

My Dear Sir—

I hope my acknowledgements for the favors bestowed upon me by the representatives of Florida, their worthy Governor and the honorable society have been in due time received. It is to me a great additional happiness to my inexpressible enjoyments, during my visit through the United States, that I have since been honored with so gratifying marks of affection and esteem, from the citizens of Florida; it highly enhances the advantage I have to be their co-proprietor in that fine part of the union.

Having been informed that it might be agreeable to the inhabitants of Tallahassee to become proprietors of one half of the section near the Metropolis, I gave of course a ready assent to any arrangement that might suit their purpose. So, I hear the holding in one hand the totality of a township most advantageously situated, would be rather inconvenient to the population; I am fully disposed to comply with that general feeling. But as information from the U. S., namely letters from Mr. Graham and Col. McKee have been long delayed by an unusual perseverance of easterly winds, I do not know what is the present state of the question—there is however an incident which I will not lose time in submitting to you.

A respectable family living in Switzerland, have applied for my opinion respecting the facility of a settlement in Alabama or West Florida, where they might transport a number of laborers and mechanics. I have answered that in both countries, situations could be found appropriate to the exertion of white labor, to the cultivation of the vine, olive tree, and to the education of the mulberry and silkworm—that I myself, was the owner of a tract of land where I thought these advantages could be secured. And I have offered to send to Governor Murphy and to you, a series of such queries as they would please to lay down. Will you be so kind, my dear sir, to redeem my pledge by your observations on the enclosed note.

I send it without any form and leave it open; in order that Mr. Graham, Col. McKee, Gen. Dall, or any other of our friends at Washington, may also give their opinion some weeks before your answer can be obtained. It seems to me, emigration of that kind, to the southern part of the U. States, could be very beneficial to the country; I however, advise adventurers not to take my decision, before one of them has been himself on the spot.

I am happy in the opportunity to offer you, my dear sir, the high regard and grateful attachment of

Your sincere friend
LAFAYETTE.

Since Lafayette was not interested in colonizing the land himself he later sold it to speculators for a sum reported to have been one hundred thousand dollars.

13

IN WASHINGTON AT ELECTION TIME

It might have been sheer coincidence that Lafayette's visit to the United States took place during an election year, but there is little doubt that his presence and the ensuing celebrations had some influence on the American political scene in 1824 and 1825. The country had already experienced its worst period of economic depression. The land and cotton booms had collapsed in 1819 and the end of Monroe's "era of good feelings" came about when money got tight. The country was slow in recovering and the depression lasted until around 1823.

Having chosen their first Presidents from an elite group of founding fathers, Americans began to look for a more representative President and Jacksonian radicals were agitating for change. They wanted someone in the President's office who would have better understanding of their needs. Agrarians began to define their rights; wider suffrage was asked for, and the people clamored for better access to central government. More public education was needed and the universities were still available only to the privileged. The poor suffered under laws that imprisoned them for debt and there was too close a connection between moneyed interest and central government. Moreover, Monroe's period of the Presidency was a time of one-party government. Another important issue at stake was the free-soil–slave-soil problem that had preceded the Missouri Compromise.

Lafayette's assumption that American democracy was the epitome of self-government seemed to have been based on his lifelong, unwavering faith in the principle of right or wrong with no in-between shades. With the exception of the slavery issue, Lafayette undoubtedly felt that his old friends of the privileged class were better qualified to serve as Chief Executives of the United States than such men as Andrew Jackson, whose roots were in the farmer class. Levasseur certainly echoed his employer's sentiments when he said of the politics of 1824, "now it [the country] found itself obliged to open the door [of the presidency] to the ambitious and designing."

Lafayette knew his tour was influential politically. Levasseur wrote, "It was during the height of the presidential question that General Lafayette appeared on the American shores. This event, as if by enchantment, paralyzed all the electoral ardour. The newspapers, which, the evening before [Lafayette's landing], were furiously combating for their favorite candidate, now closed their long column on all party disputes, and only gave admission to the unanimous expression of the public joy and national gratitude."

It is true that Lafayette's visit knocked political material off the front pages of the papers. Men of different beliefs and principles rallied together in every town and political arguments were momentarily forgotten. However, for all his democratic ideals, Lafayette represented to the American people the old line of revolutionary heroes and the founding privileged class. He was a welcome guest at the tables of Madison, Monroe, Jefferson, and Adams. John Quincy Adams hardly left Lafayette's side through the celebrations in Philadelphia, Baltimore, and Washington. Adams' toasts and speeches honoring Lafayette were widely noted in the press, which, even though it opposed his election as President, could not fault his enthusiasm in welcoming the nation's guest. There is little doubt that Levasseur only echoed Lafayette's idea of his own importance when he wrote, "For nearly two months all the discord and excitement produced by this election, which, it was said, would engender the most disastrous consequences, were forgotten, and nothing was thought of but Lafayette and the heroes of the revolution."

Although Lafayette did not express any political opinions publicly during the period preceding the election, his proximity to the incumbent, whose choice for President was John Quincy Adams, obviously was of some influence. Also, there were many nonpolitical celebrations in his honor at which all rivals for the Presidency were thrown together, making it all the more difficult for them to create identities of their own in the minds of the electorate.

At a reception given for Lafayette in October by President Monroe, candidate William H. Crawford, senile and sick, managed to put in an appearance. Crawford was rarely seen that month in the environs of Washington. He had suffered a severe stroke and could barely pull himself out of bed. As head of the Treasury Department he had been "unavailable," and it had been rumored that he could no longer read or write and that his speech was slurred and his mind damaged. His behavior at the Lafayette reception was reported as "odd." He sat down when the President was standing and did not remove his hat. When asked to do so, he did and then promptly put it back on. When told again to take his hat off, that it was not a proper place to wear it, he again complied but said, "What, cannot I wear my hat here?" This story, rumored about Washington, was enough to place serious doubts in the minds of Crawford supporters concerning his fitness for the Presidency.

Henry Clay was another contender for the office. He was popular and a well-liked Speaker of the House and represented the western factions of the country. At another entertainment for Lafayette in Washington, on the first of January, Clay and Adams, coincidentally, were seated together and it was there that they made plans to have a conference in the near future. There was little doubt in anyone's mind that the purpose of the conference was to discuss future plans for Clay should he decide to throw his electoral votes in Congress to Adams. The meeting took place on January 9 and probably decided the eventual outcome of the election, which placed John Quincy Adams in the White House. The matter was settled by a vote of Congress one month later.

The dinner for Lafayette on New Year's Day was hosted by the Senate and the House of Representatives. Its object was to fête the General at a banquet at which representatives of the entire nation would sit down together. Mr. Gailliard, President Pro Tempore of the Senate, and Henry Clay presided. James Monroe, who had been criticized more than once for his policy of never attending public dinners, made a notable exception in this case. Andrew Jackson was one of Lafayette's official escorts to the party. Lafayette had brought all the major contenders in the election battle together to break bread and offer toasts in his honor. Meanwhile, few were aware that Adams and Clay were making plans that would lead to a political agreement that would affect American history for many years to come.

On the evening of February 9, the day Adams was chosen as President, Monroe gave a large party at which Lafayette was once again the guest of honor. As could be expected after a long and confusing election that had an outcome so agreeable to the incumbent, the crowd attending was larger than at any other dinner Lafayette had previously attended at the White House. Levasseur wrote, "All the inhabitants of Washington were attracted by the desire of seeing the president elect and his competitors, who, it was taken for granted, would be present, and who, in fact, were so, with the exception of Mr. Crawford, who was detained at home by illness." Levasseur was amazed upon seeing the greeting given by General Jackson to President-Elect Adams. "The moment they perceived each other, they hastened to meet, taking each other cordially by the hand. The congratulations offered by General Jackson were open and sincere; Mr. Adams appeared to be deeply moved, and the numerous witnesses could not restrain the expression of their satisfaction. Mr. Clay arrived an instant afterwards, and the same scene was repeated."

In view of recent Presidential history, another observation of Levasseur's on the American Presidency should be noted:

It will be seen that the constitution, in fixing in a precise manner the duties and power of the chief magistrate, has rather kept in view the welfare and interests of the nation, than in the gratification on one individual and his family. Hence, the president is placed in such a situation, that whatever may be his personal character, it is impossible for him to injure the liberty, right, or honour of his fellow citizens. He does not, like some kings on the old continent, enjoy several millions of revenue, and immense estates. The law only allows him $25,000 dollars as a salary, but it is not by the sumptuousness of his equipages, by the splendour of a numerous guard, or by the numbers of his courtiers that he maintains the dignity of his station.

14

JOURNEY THROUGH THE CAROLINAS

The winter months in Washington in 1824–25 were certainly pleasant and rewarding for Lafayette. The General was, for the first time in many years, free from concern about money and he knew that the generous gift of Congress brought with it the good wishes of the entire nation. He could take some satisfaction in the outcome of the election and knew that while the country might be divided on many issues, it was not divided in its affection for him. He was a frequent guest at the home of the President and always in demand as guest of honor at important social events.

Invitations came into him at a rapid rate and it was obvious that once having accepted the gifts of the people, Lafayette had an obligation to them. The southern and western states were especially adamant in their requests that they be given an opportunity to entertain him and by the first of February elaborate plans were laid to begin a journey that would enable Lafayette to visit all of the remaining states and still be in Boston by June 17, the date he had promised to assist in the celebration of the anniversary of the battle of Bunker Hill.

Lafayette and his fellow travelers were well aware of the hardships to be encountered in a journey through the undeveloped portion of the United States. While the steamboat system was well-established on the major rivers of the Midwest, roads were bad and in some areas still nonexistent. Parts of the country through which the party must travel were still unsettled and passage in many places probably would have to be on horseback, an uncomfortable mode of travel Lafayette had so far been able to avoid.

George Lafayette and Auguste Levasseur were largely responsible for planning the southern and western tours. Washingtonians who were familiar with the frontier and Postmaster General McLean especially were very helpful. By planning the trip carefully in advance and arranging to adhere to an itinerary and time-table as closely as possible Lafayette was assured that, barring any serious accidents or sickness, he would be able to complete the journey and fulfill his promise to his Boston friends.

Many Washington friends of the General expressed their fears that the trip would be too strenuous and that he was foolish to expose himself to the dangers that lay outside of what they considered "civilization." A strong carriage was provided for the difficult roads and care was taken to purchase good saddle horses to be used in areas where the carriage could not pass. Baggage was reduced to a minimum.

Meanwhile, while others worked to complete plans for the next tour, Lafayette was not inactive. He visited old friends and made trips to Baltimore, to Alexandria and Arlington, Virginia, and to Harrisburg, Pennsylvania. He appeared at the theater often and on January 17 attended an exposition of his portrait that the artist Ary Scheffer had presented to Congress. On his last night in the capital he went to a Washington's birthday ball with James Monroe and John Quincy Adams.

On the twenty-third of February, at nine in the evening, Lafayette, Levasseur, George, and the servant, Bastien, embarked on the steamship *Potomac* and after two days and a night they landed at Norfolk, Virginia, and went to Suffolk where there were welcoming festivities.

Lafayette's entry into North Carolina was less dignified than his jubilant marches into more populated areas. After leaving Suffolk and stopping to dine at Somerton, he continued on toward Murfreesboro. However, the bad condition of the road so exhausted the horses that they became mired down outside of the town. Since Lafayette had been expected, the town was highly illuminated, and as soon as his party was sighted the cannons roared and the gunfire rang loudly through the night air. All this tumult did not inspire the horses to get up and for a while it appeared that the celebration in Murfreesboro might have to be postponed. After much prodding by the drivers the horses finally stood on their feet for Lafayette's entry into town. That night he wrote home to his family, "My health bears up well under the journey."

The next day, a Sunday, the travelers continued on to Halifax, where they crossed the Roanoke River by ferryboat. The following morning they were expected in Raleigh, where Governor Burton and a company of volunteer dragoons, which had marched one hundred and fifty miles in the rain, awaited the hero.

On the morning of Lafayette's arrival in Raleigh a serious accident took place. In one of the calashes following Lafayette's carriage rode General Daniel and a young officer of his staff. The driver lost control of the horses and the runaway dashed the carriage against the trunk of a tree. The riders were thrown out of the calash and Daniel was badly injured. The procession was stopped immediately and Lafayette walked back to the scene of the accident to see if there was anything he could do. Daniel was beginning to gain consciousness, but General Williams, lancet in hand, was about to bleed him. George Lafayette begged Williams to desist, saying that to bleed anyone so soon after he had eaten might have injurious consequences. Daniel was then taken to a nearby plantation and the next day was fully recovered. He expressed his warmest thanks to George for having saved him from a "cure" that might have proved fatal. The French visitors were aware that bloodletting was used all too frequently in the United States, where there was a shortage of physicians. Levasseur commented, "The amateurs tended to do it much too profusely."

On the second of March the already eventful day ended with a reception by the students of the University of North Carolina and a public dinner and ball. Lafayette slept that night in Government House, held a reception the next morning for the small population of Raleigh, breakfasted with Colonel Polk, and by early afternoon had left for Fayetteville.

Lafayette's entry into Fayetteville was accompanied by torrents of rain. This did not deter the men of the town from lining up along the road for many miles, while the women of Fayetteville waited in the town and made preparations for the visit. Dressed in their best they scurried around busily in the rain. Unfortunately, an open platform had been erected in the center of the town for the welcoming speeches and everyone stood in the downpour while Chief Justice Troomer recapitulated all of the obligations that America had to Lafayette and retraced the General's persecutions at the hands of his Austrian captors.

When he was finally led to his quarters Lafayette was told, "You are here in your own town, in your own house, surrounded by your own children. Dispose of all—everything is yours." The bad weather persisted as the volunteer militia companies maneuvered in front of Lafayette's quarters. Upon his departure from Fayetteville on Saturday, March 5, after many parties and celebrations, he dismounted and shook each soldier affectionately by the hand to show his gratitude for their most uncomfortable duty.

In addition to a large part of Fayetteville's citizens, who escorted Lafayette's party until nightfall, there were also members of the Committee on Arrangements from Cheraw, South Carolina, who had come to Fayetteville to escort the hero into their town. The South Carolina border was reached twenty-four hours later and fresh horses and carriages were provided. Although Lafayette did not arrive at Cheraw until eleven at night, the fifteen hundred citizens of the town were all waiting to form a procession and to display an illumination of their town. The following morning Lafayette received the citizens of the town and reviewed the military. He left at noon for Camden.

The roads to Camden were, in places, impassable because the

60. Liberty cap, of carved wood and polychromed, was used on pole as parade ornament during Lafayette's visit to America. *E. Norman Flayderman Collection*

rains had brought considerable flooding, and often logs had to be laid over the marshes so that the horses and carriages could pass. Lafayette's escort became divided and when darkness fell the group was still in wilderness and the carriages scattered. By ten o'clock the carriage in which George and Auguste were riding was separated from the rest, and after hearing a loud crash and feeling a violent shock the passengers discovered that their carriage tongue was broken. The two dragoon guards that were their escort gave up their own horses to the two visitors and led them into a campsite built outside of an isolated house, where Lafayette had arrived an hour earlier. Fires were lighted and a trumpet sounded throughout the night to bring the scattered procession together.

In the morning Lafayette and his secretary were able to survey the house and area in which they had spent the night. They were in the midst of what Levasseur called "a new settlement" and he described the dwelling that was typical of frontier homes of 1825:

The house in which we had passed the night was the only dwelling in the place, and it was still unfinished. By its side they had begun to raise the frames of some other buildings, doubtless intended for granaries and stables. Numerous trunks of half hewn trees collected together showed that it was the intention of the owner soon to erect other buildings, and already the forest was prostrated to a considerable extent. But a few vast trees were standing in the clearing, whose branches were not only lopped off, but some of them were deprived of their bark, and blackened for their whole length by the action of the flames which had been employed to burn the brush about them.

As Lafayette was given a tour of the area it was explained to him that this was the way all American towns started and that the little town of Cheraw had begun the same way only three or four years previously. He was shown the fenced-in acreage and the cattle, sheep, and hogs owned by the farmer. It was explained that the hogs provided the major sustenance while the land was being cleared for crops, but before the farmer had his own crops he had to find something to trade for the food that he did not yet grow. Therefore, he was obliged to tap the enormous pine trees in the surrounding forest for turpentine. The dead trees yielded tar, and as the trees were cleared, they provided products that could be sold. As the cleared land increased and other settlers saw that the area would sustain them through the first dismal years, they staked claims on surrounding property. In this way, it was explained, towns grew from wilderness.

The procession was reformed that morning and continued in the daylight through the pine forests and sandy marshes to Camden, South Carolina. The weather had cleared and spring was in the air. Camden's two hundred citizens and the population from the surrounding countryside welcomed Lafayette, who had come the distance to participate in the laying of a cornerstone of a monument to be built to the memory of Baron de Kalb, the German soldier who had come to aid in the Revolution and died after having been wounded eleven times.

On Wednesday, March 9, Lafayette left Camden to go to Columbia, but upon arriving at the outskirts of the town he was asked to delay his entrance until the following day because arrangements had not been completed. The group stayed twelve miles outside Columbia and arrived in town the next afternoon, where Lafayette was received with great pomp and ceremony. The streets were ornamented with flags and numerous triumphal arches, on one of which three girls were stationed with flags inscribed in gold, "Lafayette," "de Kalb," and "Pulaski." Lafayette was welcomed by the mayor and Governor Manning and also heard an address by a student of South Carolina College. A grand ball was held in the evening and the next morning Lafayette set out for Charleston.

It began to rain again when the travelers were in the midst of a thick forest and the way was dark and dangerous. Levasseur's carriage again broke down and he, George, and others were forced to wait while servants found and lighted pine torches to guide them to the house where they were to spend the night.

After only a few hours' sleep an escort of cavalry arrived from Charleston and all set out together through the thick pine forests. There is little doubt that all were relieved to see the town of Charleston, as Levasseur's following comment illustrates:

Our eyes now rested with pleasure upon clusters of verdant and beautifully shaped saplings among which superb magnolias were majestically elevated. The entrance to the city appeared to us like a delicious garden. The coolness of the night had condensed the perfumes from the orange, peach and almond trees, covered with flowers, and embalmed the air.

On the outskirts of the town they changed carriages, formed a procession, and on a signal from cannons marched into Charleston. The town had been the first settlement to receive Lafayette, when as a youth he had come in the defense of liberty. It therefore held a special place of honor among the hundreds of towns and cities that paid homage to the hero that year. The militia of the entire state was represented in the long procession into the city and many of the men had marched fifty miles a day to join in the celebration on Monday, March 14. Among the military groups was a corps of Frenchmen dressed in uniforms copied from those of Lafayette's National Guard of Paris and this company was given the place of honor in the parade, that of escorting Lafayette's carriage.

The Charleston line of march included representatives of the clergy, the Society of the Cincinnati, veterans of the Revolutionary War, students and teachers from the various schools of the states, officers of the United States Army and Navy, judges of the various courts, children of the public schools, members of the German, French, Jewish, and Hibernian beneficent societies, and representatives of the trades. The remainder of the citizens followed the procession on horseback and foot and the cries of "Welcome Lafayette!" were said to have drowned out the band music. Added to this was the thunder of cannon from the ships in port and the ringing of all the town bells.

In all, Lafayette spent three days in Charleston and all balls, banquets, ceremonies, and speeches were shared with another guest of honor, Colonel Francis Huger, a Charlestonian who had made a vain attempt to free Lafayette from Olmütz Prison. Lafayette was given many keepsakes of value, among which was a miniature portrait of Colonel Huger painted by Mr. Frazer and with a frame of solid gold made in Philadelphia. Levasseur commented that the frame would have done honor to the most experienced French jewelers. Another gift was a map of the state enclosed in a case of silver.

15

THE GUEST OF SAVANNAH

In order to spare Lafayette further travel on South Carolina's poor roads the Charleston Committee arranged to have him go by sea to his next destination, Savannah, Georgia. On March 17 Lafayette embarked at Fitzsimmon's wharf on the steamship *Henry Shultz.* The shore and vessels in the harbor were crowded with the citizens of Charleston who came to bid farewell to Lafayette as his boat drifted toward Sullivan's Island and Fort Moultrie. A salute was fired as Lafayette's boat passed the fort.

The *Henry Shultz* entered port at Edisto Island, where Lafayette could remain only a few hours. The islanders were all gathered at a dockside public house, and when told that the visit would be short, they crowded all the entertainments they had planned to fit into the available time. "We had," wrote Levasseur, "at the same time, the harangue, the public dinner, the ball, and even the baptism of a charming little infant, to which the name of Lafayette was given." After this confusion Lafayette and his party quickly traversed the island in a carriage and then departed.

Throughout the remainder of the voyage to Savannah the boat steamed in and out among the small coastal islands. It was nearly midnight when the *Henry Shultz* passed Beaufort, where the shouts of the people lined along the shore woke the sleeping passengers. The crowd insisted on seeing Lafayette and he awoke and made a brief appearance in the town. The visit, however, included a formal reception, an artillery salute, and a parade.

Lafayette's visit to Savannah had been planned and anticipated for months by its citizens. Even before he had reached the shores of the United States the people of Savannah had adopted a resolution to invite him to their city. The invitation was sent on August 5 and renewed after Washington's birthday, when the southern tour was announced. A letter written by Lafayette on February 20 and received by the mayor of Savannah on the twenty-eighth made it clear that the city would have an opportunity to be host to the hero:

My Dear Sir,

My route, upon which several friends have had the goodness to consult together, is at last fixed, and makes me arrive at Charleston on the 13th. March, to leave it on the 16th for Savannah, Augusta and Milledgeville. I will avail myself of the Steam Boat as much as I can. The pressure of time; an engagement at Boston for the 17th June, which I would be truly unhappy to disappoint; and other considerations relative to my American visit, and family avocations in Europe, make it impossible for me to lessen the rapidity of my march, and very thankful for the means to expedite it. Enclosed you will find my letter to the Governor of Georgia.

Receive my best thanks
and affectionate regard.
LAFAYETTE

Fortunately, the city of Savannah published a souvenir booklet describing all the events that took place and the arrangements that had to be made. It is interesting to find out the way in which a city banded together to prepare the complicated arrangements for the hero's visit. As soon as a firm date was established a citizens' committee was formed of the authorities of the city, private citizens, and officers of the First Regiment of the Georgia Hussars. These three groups, called the "Lafayette Committee," were charged with making all preparations for the reception. Accommodations were provided for Lafayette and the governor at a mansion owned by a Mrs. Maxwell, and Colonel Huger was invited to attend.

Even though Lafayette was expected to arrive at Savannah the

AN ACCOUNT

OF THE

RECEPTION OF

GENERAL LAFAYETTE

IN SAVANNAH;

ON SATURDAY, MARCH 19th, 1825.

OF THE ENTERTAINMENTS GIVEN HIM;

AND OF

THE CEREMONIES,

MASONIC & CIVIC,

ON LAYING THE CORNER STONES OF

MONUMENTS

TO THE MEMORY OF

GENERALS GREENE AND PULASKI.

SAVANNAH:
W. T. WILLIAMS.
1825.

61. Title page of souvenir book giving an account of Lafayette's visit to Savannah, Georgia, in 1825. *Benjamin DeForest Curtiss Collection, Watertown Library*

actual plans did not begin until the final week and frenzied preparations preceded the visit. It was not known at exactly what hour the *Shultz* would appear and the excitement built as stages and packets from surrounding areas brought many strangers into the city. The troops reached town the day before the arrival and parties were held in the city in anticipation of the great event. A false alarm at five-thirty on Saturday morning that the steamboat had been sighted called the military to several parade grounds and a line was formed by eight o'clock, but since it was nowhere in sight the troops were temporarily dismissed. All boats in the harbor were decked out with flags and pennants.

A temporary landing was erected at the wharf, and when the steamboat finally came into view the Committee on Arrangements boarded three barges decorated with flags to go to Fort Jackson, where they would board the *Shultz* in order to disembark at Savannah with Lafayette. The *Shultz* arrived with the band playing and all guns firing and when Lafayette was rowed into shore he was met by a huge crowd and a welcoming committee that included officers from every organization in Savannah.

As Lafayette placed his foot upon the landing platform a salute was fired by the Chatham Artillery and six cheers were given by the citizens. After some welcoming speeches Lafayette ascended the bluff and was again cheered as he was presented to Governor Troup, who made the major welcoming address. Lafayette responded and was then introduced to several Revolutionary soldiers, one of whom, Captain Rees, said, "I remember you! I saw you in Philadelphia!" Lafayette took the old captain's hand between his own and replied, "Ah! I remember!"

Lafayette was introduced to the officers of the brigade and the regiment while a salute was fired along the whole line of infantry. He then reviewed the troops and acended his carriage for the procession, which included fifteen sections, and it was five-thirty in the afternoon when he was finally taken to his lodgings. The troops then filed off to the south common and fired a national salute, after which they returned to the quarters of Lafayette, where they paid a marching salute. At sundown another salute was fired by the volunteer marine corps.

The evening's banquet, originally scheduled for four o'clock, did not start until seven. It was held in the Council Chamber, which was decorated with arches, branches, and banners. In the window in back of Lafayette's chair was a large transparency representing the General, over which a scroll was inscribed, "He fought for us." In the opposite window was a transparent portrait of Washington with the inscription "The Father of His Country." In another window was an allegorical transparency representing a monument surmounted by a bust of Lafayette. The hero's toast to Savannah was, "The City of Savannah—and may her young prosperity more and more show to the old world, the superiority of Republican institutions' self government."

Thirteen official toasts were drunk and eighteen "volunteer toasts" were made before Lafayette retired. The hardier guests stayed on for twenty more toasts drunk to, among others, "the civic arrangements of this day," "the inhabitants of La Grange," and "Andrew Jackson." During the banquet a beautiful illumination was held throughout the city. The Exchange glowed with variegated lamps and the City Hotel exhibited a large, lighted transparency. The Lafayette Coffee House displayed a transparency of the "Landing of Lafayette at Georgetown" and other stores and houses were similarly decorated. Although the city celebrated far into the night and was crowded with strangers from surrounding areas no accidents occurred and, as far as is known, no crimes were committed.

The next day, Sunday, Lafayette held a reception for the French citizens of Savannah in the morning and dined with the governor and invited guests, including the Committee of Arrangement. He received citizens in the Council Chamber that evening but the ball held in his honor went on without him. He retired early.

The people of Savannah wanted to pay tribute to the memories of two of its Revolutionary heroes, General Nathanael Greene and Brigadier Count Pulaski, during Lafayette's visit and elaborate plans had been made for the General to assist in laying cornerstones for two monuments to be erected, Greene's in Johnston's Square and Pulaski's in Chippewa Square.

On Monday, March 21, the several Masonic lodges of the area formed a procession at their Grand Lodge Room at nine in the morning. Accompanied by a band of music they marched to Lafayette's lodgings, where the General, his suite, and the governor joined the march to the site of Greene's proposed monument. The procession was bright and colorful with all the members of the fraternal order dressed in the full robes and regalia of their offices and carrying banners. When the procession reached its destination five hundred schoolchildren, each carrying a basket of flowers, threw the blossoms in Lafayette's path. The cornerstone was laid to the accompaniment of many speeches and specially composed music. The original order of the procession was again formed and the scene was repeated at the site of Pulaski's memorial.

Following these ceremonies Lafayette assisted a Mrs. Harden at the presentation of a flag that she had embroidered, with Lafayette's portrait worked into the design, to the first regiment of the Georgia militia. He attended a banquet at three that afternoon and at five boarded the steamboat *Altamaha* accompanied by his traveling companions, the governor of Georgia and the Committee on Arrangements.

16

THE TREK THROUGH ALABAMA

Lafayette's next destination was Augusta, Georgia, and the *Altamaha* steamed some sixty miles through marshy, low ground. On Wednesday, March 23, at four in the afternoon, the boat was met by two other steamboats crowded with citizens of Augusta, who welcomed the hero with three loud cheers. This was answered by the band of musicians aboard the *Altamaha,* which played a lively rendition of *Yankee Doodle.* The three boats ascended the river together, each captain attempting to get the most speed out of his boat. "There was something frightful in this contest," wrote Levasseur. "The three roaring vessels seemed to fly in the midst of black clouds of smoke, which prevented us from seeing each other." The *Altamaha* was the victor and its captain, who was described as "a man who would blow up his vessel rather than be beaten on such an occasion," was ecstatic.

Despite the grand reception into Augusta, Lafayette had planned to spend only one day there so that he would maintain his schedule. However, so many entertainments had been arranged that he yielded to the entreaties of the citizens and stayed an extra day. The celebrations did not stop for forty-eight hours and for the first time Lafayette showed signs of exhaustion. According to his secretary, "he suffered a fatigue which caused us a momenatry inquietude."

The General, George, and Auguste were pleased to find in Augusta a friend, a Mr. King, who had been a passenger with them on the *Cadmus*. The most difficult part of the journey lay ahead and Mr. King arranged to send messages to France for Lafayette and to help lighten the baggage and send the extra effects to France as well. This included all the gifts that Lafayette had collected during his southern tour. Levasseur wrote, "We foresaw that we were going to travel the worst roads that we had yet encountered since leaving Washington."

On Thursday Lafayette crossed the Savannah River and visited the interesting village of Hamburg. This was a planned town of one hundred houses, all built within the same week and inhabited within two months. In the evening he returned to Augusta to attend a reception at City Hall, a public dinner, and a ball.

The following day, still suffering from fatigue, Lafayette took to the road to visit the towns of Milledgeville, Warrenton, and Sparta. The roads were as bad as expected and part of the trip had to be made on horseback. On the first day of the trip the General's carriage was so shaken that it made him ill, but he recovered after spending the night in Warrenton. The following night he was in Sparta.

Milledgeville was reached at noon on March 27 and Lafayette was escorted by cavalry from Baldwin County. The celebrations included an illumination in the evening and the *Milledgeville Patriot* reported that "six pocketbooks were stolen during the welcoming ceremonies, one containing $4500.00." The town was the capital of Georgia at this time and all official honors were paid to Lafayette by city and state representatives. The ball held in the evening was so crowded that no one could dance and Lafayette, although he had been sick and was to travel at a very early hour the next morning, remained well into the night.

Governor Troup assigned aides-de-camp to accompany Lafayette through the territory inhabited by the Creek Indians. The first night out was spent in the new village of Macon, but once out of the vicinity of the town the group was in virgin forest and the road they traveled on was no more than a kind of gulley or fissure.

George and Auguste rode on horseback, but it was thought best to have Lafayette remain in his carriage, which had to be picked up and carried in some places. They arrived without incident in the early evening at Moss's Trading Camp, where Lafayette was disappointed to find out that the tribe of Indians he had expected to greet him there had grown impatient and moved elsewhere along the route.

The first day into the interior became extremely difficult. Thirty-two miles over roads that were little more than footpaths and a violent storm made the route treacherous and the group took shelter in a cabin along the way. The cabin already was occupied by some Indian hunters who were drying their clothes by the fire and the weary French visitors sat down among them unrecognized. Levasseur, who was very eager to learn something about American Indians, attempted to converse with them in sign language. The indifference of the Indians stymied the secretary until he used the universal language of the brandy bottle, which the Indians promptly accepted and emptied. Levasseur felt that they parted on rather good terms.

As soon as the storm subsided the travelers continued on until they reached a group of log cabins owned by an American fur trader. Two male Indians were sitting in the dooryard and Levasseur described them as "remarkable for their beauty and form." They were both dressed in short frocks of a light material gathered at the waist by a wampum belt and the younger of the two spoke excellent English. He said he had been educated in the United States, but had come back to Indian territory when he discovered he preferred the Indian way of life to that of the white man. Levasseur and George made friends with the younger Indian, whose name was Hamley, and were invited to visit his home. Hamley demonstrated Indian dances and Levasseur reciprocated by doing the French dances that he knew.

On Thursday, March 31, the group plunged deeper and deeper into the forests and the French travelers became more impressed with the ways of the Indians they saw and more depressed by the manner in which they had been treated by "civilized man." Levasseur was forced to admit, however, that the treaties with the Indians, no matter how unfair, had been made by negotiation rather than extermination, and he said that the white man's treatment of the Indian in America could not compare to the crimes of Great Britain in India.

When the group reached the banks of the Chattahoochee River, which divides the states of Georgia and Alabama, a full Indian delegation under the leadership of Chief Chilly McIntosh was there to greet him along with the Alabama Committee on Arrangements. This reception of Lafayette differed markedly from those he had received elsewhere in the United States. There were no cannons or bells. The women and children were lined up along the river's bank and cries of joy were heard when the onlookers first sighted Lafayette's carriage being ferried across from the Georgia side. Indian men were stationed on a hill above the banks of the river and rushed to the edge as soon as Lafayette was sighted.

George was the first to disembark and he was immediately surrounded by Indians, who touched him and his clothing and danced and leaped about him. As the rest of the party began to reach shore the chief gave a loud cry, which was answered by the entire assemblage. Then everyone fell silent as Lafayette's foot touched the shore. Some of the Indians seized the General's carriage and insisted that Lafayette get back in so that he would not have to walk in the mud. They then carried the carriage a safe distance from shore and set it down gently.

Chief McIntosh approached Lafayette and in English said that all his brethren were happy in being visited by one who, in his affection for the inhabitants of America, had never made a distinction of blood and color; that Lafayette was the honored father of all the races of men dwelling on that continent. As the chief finished his speech all the male Indians advanced and placed their right arm on that of Lafayette in a token of friendship. The General's carriage, still carrying its illustrious passenger, was then lifted up the hill to the Indian village.

Like Hamley, Chilly McIntosh had been educated in white schools. Levasseur wrote that the young chief seemed depressed and blamed it at first on the fact that his father had made a notoriously unfavorable treaty with the white man. Later, Levasseur came to the conclusion that the Indian's depression was caused by the circumstance that "his mind had been cultivated at the expense of his happiness." From conversations with the Indian, Levasseur deduced that he appreciated the real situation of his nation, saw it rapidly becoming weaker, and foresaw its speedy destruction. He admitted that it was impossible to overcome the wandering nature of his people and felt that instead of benefiting from a nearness to "civilization" he knew that it was only a means of introducing vices that heretofore had been alien to his people.

The Indians, upon approaching their village, removed most of their clothing, painted their faces, and announced there would be a mock battle in honor of the "white father." The war games were played with a ball and racquets and the young chief's team won. After this, Lafayette visited some of the huts and the Indian school.

When Lafayette was ready to continue his journey Chilly McIntosh appeared dressed in white-man's clothing and requested permission to accompany the General to Montgomery. He wanted to take his ten-year-old brother to a citizen of that town who had promised to educate the boy. All set out together for Haynes Crabtree Tavern, three miles west on Uchee Creek.

While Lafayette rested at the cabin Levasseur visited the local Indian tribe with McIntosh and both tried their skill with the bow and arrow. Levasseur said of the Indian's ability, "He had the arm and eye of William Tell." On their way back to the tavern the two met up with an Indian chief on horseback. The Indian's wife sat behind him on the horse and remained there while the Indian dismounted to go into the tavern, approach Lafayette, and make a few purchases. When he came out the Indian woman brought the horse to her husband and held the bridle and stirrup for him. Then she jumped up behind him and they rode off.

Levasseur asked McIntosh if this was the general condition of all females of the Indian nation and was told that it was. The women cultivated the ground, carried the game for the hunters, and loaded all cooking utensils and household articles taken on the tribe's wanderings. Even maternal cares did not exonerate women from these occupations. Later, after having observed many more Indian women in the Uchee Creek area, Levasseur concluded that their condition was not as bad as he had been led to expect. He said he never saw any signs of harshness or abuse by Indians toward their women.

On their journey the next day from Crabtree Tavern to the cabin of the Big Warrior, the group met several parties of Indians who helped in extricating Lafayette's small carriage from dangerous places in the road. It was the flood season and on one occasion a stream had risen above the wooden bridge over which the General's carriage had to cross. Indians lined up on either side of the bridge and formed human chains to mark the edges of the bridge. Their only reward was an opportunity for each Indian to take the General by the hand. They called him their "White Father," "the Envoy of the Great Spirit," and the "Great Warrior from France." McIntosh acted as interpreter and returned Lafayette's good wishes and gratitude.

After a night spent at Big Warrior, Lafayette arrived the next evening at Line Creek. This was a frontier trading village, which the Frenchmen found unpleasant because of the advantage being taken of the Indians. Levasseur accused the town's citizens of poisoning the Indians with intoxicating liquors and he called them the cruelest and most dangerous enemies of the Indian nations. Both Lafayette and his secretary, after observing several incidents at Line Creek, had cause to agree with George Washington, who had said, "Whenever I have been called upon to decide between an

Indian and a white man, I have always found that the white was the aggressor."

On the third of April Lafayette left Line Creek and was escorted to Montgomery, where he was received by Governor Israel Pickens and many citizens. The travelers were entertained at the home of Colonel John Edmondson and in the evening a ball was held at Freeney's Tavern. George and Auguste reluctantly parted company with Chilly McIntosh, who had become a good friend, and at two in the morning embarked on the steamboat *Anderson,* which would take them down the Alabama River. The boat had been luxuriously fitted out for Lafayette's use and it was provided with a band of musicians sent from New Orleans. The ladies of Montgomery came on board to wish Lafayette a safe voyage, and as the boat was getting up steam many bonfires were set on shore.

17

UP THE MISSISSIPPI
TO ST. LOUIS

The trip down the Alabama River was described as "delicious." Happy to be off their horses, Lafayette and his companions enjoyed the wooded shores of the river and three days of music provided by the Louisiana band, although it had a limited repertoire and repeated the same few patriotic airs throughout the journey. On Monday, April 4, the steamboat stopped at Cahaba, where lavish entertainments had been planned. The next day it anchored at Selma for a reception, dinner, and a Masonic visit. The group reembarked at eleven in the evening and continued its journey until noon the next day, when it arrived at Claiborne for entertainments that lasted until midafternoon.

On April 7, the boat, after covering three hundred miles in three days, arrived in Mobile Bay. Without steam the journey would have taken a month to six weeks. Mobile, the oldest city in the state, had a population of eighteen hundred, all of whom set up a loud cheer as Lafayette's boat came in sight. Lafayette was welcomed under a great triumphal arch adorned with flags of Mexico, the republics of South America, Greece, and the United States. He was then led to an immense hall, where he was introduced to all the ladies of the town and greeted by the governor of Alabama. The people of Mobile had made elaborate plans for a lengthy visit from Lafayette and were disappointed when he told them that he was obliged to be in New Orleans as soon as possible. After a public dinner, a ball, and a Masonic celebration Lafayette boarded the steamboat *Natchez* for Louisiana.

The *Natchez,* commanded by Captain Davis, had been sent by the city of New Orleans to carry Lafayette to the shores of the Mississippi and on it were the Louisiana deputation and Mr. Duplantier, an old friend and companion-in-arms to Lafayette. The sound of cannon at daybreak announced that the boat was about to weigh anchor and Lafayette came on deck to receive the farewell of Mobile's population. By nightfall the boat was out of Mobile Bay and well into the Gulf of Mexico.

The route taken was a direct one across the gulf. Less-assured captains might have taken the safer coastline route and Captain Davis soon had cause to rue his bold decision. A severe storm arose and all the passengers became seasick. The waves were so high during the night that many of the cabins were inundated. By morning Lafayette's secretary was surprised to find that he was still alive and he arrived on deck in time to see the boat enter the Mississippi delta. He noted the dismal appearance of the area, the decaying tree trunks, and enormous alligators "of menacing appearance." The Mississippi, he said, was more like a sea than a river, with distant shores and tumultuous waves. That night the captain cast anchor and everyone got some necessary rest.

The following day the voyage resumed in the early afternoon. It was Sunday, April 10. The current had subsided by this time and the river narrowed. As the boat passed Fort Planquemine it was given a thirteen-gun salute and late that afternoon the passengers could perceive the walls of New Orleans. This was a welcome sight; for sixty miles they had seen little else besides cypress trees covered with Spanish Beard. Levasseur noted that Louisianans used this strange plant for mattress stuffing and also mixed it with mortar as a building material.

As Lafayette prepared to disembark cries of *"Vive la Liberte,"* *"Vive l'ami de l'Amerique,"* and *"Vive Lafayette"* were heard from the populace on shore. It was still raining heavily, but the spirits of the crowd were not dampened as Lafayette was enthusiastically greeted by many of his own countrymen.

After welcoming speeches in which the governor of Louisiana depicted Frenchmen enjoying a liberty in New Orleans that was still problematical in their own country, crowds forced their way into the building, Andrew Jackson's old quarters, in order to be presented to Lafayette. The Revolutionary veterans were among them and Lafayette held many reunions with those he had known. Despite the storm outside, the line of march into the city was formed.

The procession passed slowly through two lines of troops and dense crowds, and as Lafayette went through on foot, bells were rung, artillery sounded, and the rain pelted everyone. The procession finally came to a halt at the Place d'Arms, where a great triumphal arch, sixty feet high, had been erected. After the ceremonies Lafayette was escorted to the Cabildo, or City Hall, renamed "Lafayette House" in his honor. He then reviewed troops from his balcony and this was followed by a review of a group of one hundred Choctaw Indians. The General was gratified that the allies of the Americans in the Seminole War had been included in the ceremonies.

During the stay in New Orleans Lafayette attended special performances given at the American and French theaters. Although, as in New York, special material had been written pertaining to the hero's life and particularly to his imprisonment at Olmütz, the actors had little opportunity to perform as planned. During the week the General received representatives of many New Orleans groups, among them the bar, the clergy, the militia, the Medical Society, free blacks, and Spanish citizens. Banquets and military reviews rounded out the visit.

At dawn on Friday, the fifteenth, Lafayette set out on foot across the parade grounds and got into the carriage to be taken to his place of embarkation. The *Natchez* waited in the river and the entire population of New Orleans watched in silence as the steamboat pulled away. Officials of the city and state accompanied Lafayette upriver for two miles and then most of them boarded a boat to return home.

Twenty-four hours after leaving New Orleans the *Natchez* arrived at Duncan's Point, eight miles downriver from Baton Rouge, and picked up the delegation from that city. The room prepared for Lafayette's reception in that town was decorated with busts of Jackson and Washington crowned with flowers and laurel wreaths. A public dinner was held and that evening the few remaining citizens of New Orleans who had stayed on the *Natchez* left to return home. The next segment of Lafayette's voyage would be too lengthy for them to remain.

The steamboat chugged up the Mississippi River to Natchez, a distance of two hundred and sixty miles, in thirty-two hours. The passage was pleasant and many boats and barges were sighted along the way. Levasseur noted that the most interesting of these was a square boat that had neither sails, masts, or oars. It floated down the river at the mercy of the currents and looked like an enormous box. This type of craft was called an "ark" and was used by Kentuckians to transport grain, poultry, and cattle. When the arks reached New Orleans, where the cargoes were sold, the owners dismantled the boats, sold the lumber, and then hiked back home.

On Monday, April 18, discharges of cannon were heard at dawn and the rooftops of Natchez could be seen from the steamboat. Lafayette was taken ashore at Bacon's Landing, where a calash and four horses waited with an escort of infantry and cavalry. The landing outside of the city had been chosen so that Lafayette could view the countryside on his entrance into the town. As the carriage advanced all citizens along the route joined the procession and welcoming ceremonies were held on the highest point overlooking the river.

As Lafayette was being escorted to his hotel he noticed a long line of children led by Colonel Marshall, of Natchez. He asked Lafayette to shake hands with all the children of the town, and Levasseur, witnessing this scene along with the proud parents, observed that the parents congratulated each other on the happy influence this day would have on the future characters of their offspring. After Lafayette left America a legend grew that any little girl who had been kissed by Lafayette would grow up to be a great beauty. Doubtless the parents of all girls thus honored felt there was truth to the legend.

Although Lafayette spent only twenty-four hours in Natchez the celebrations included a ball that lasted until daybreak, at which time Lafayette, George, and Auguste finally were able to leave. "In leaving Natchez," noted Levasseur, "we parted as it were from the civilized world." Between Natchez and St. Louis the steamboat did not pass a single group of houses that deserved the name of town or village. The banks of the Mississippi presented nothing but overflown flat edges and thick forests. The swarms of mosquitoes settled in thick clouds around the passengers, and someone, fortunately, had had the foresight to provide netting for the beds.

At this point the river was as monotonous as the scenery and there were evidences of disaster and devastation along the route. The ravages of a previous hurricane and the resulting uprooted giant trees added to the problems of navigation. The roots of trees, unseen in the water, could pierce the bottom of a boat, and woodchoppers along the way who provided fuel for the *Natchez* told of an explosion in the boiler of a steamboat that had caused the death of the forty passengers on board. Many boats, crippled by holes caused by snags, were seen being repaired along the river banks.

Regardless of the obvious hazards of steaming up the Mississippi River in 1825, Lafayette had good reason to feel secure. The vessel was skillfully managed and fitted with all the delicacies that might appeal to the General and his party. Members of various deputations were on board and all seemed to be having a good time. The boat chugged up the river, passing on the left Louisiana, Arkansas, and Missouri, and on the right Mississippi, Tennessee, and Kentucky. The only stops it made were to take in wood, and in most cases, when fuel was needed, there were woodsmen along the way from whom the captain could purchase it. When no woodsman could be found the captain sent his own men to cut the necessary quantity of logs. When this happened, the captain nailed to the trunk of a tree a note upon which was written the number of cords taken, the name of the boat, the captain's place of residence, the date of passage, and the captain's signature. The owner of the property would then send a bill, and obviously any show of bad faith would make it impossible for a captain to obtain fuel on future runs.

At the mouth of the Ohio River the pilot of the *Natchez* refused to continue farther up the Mississippi because he was not familiar with that part of the river and was unwilling to endanger the life of the illustrious guest. Captain Davis therefore took his boat into the Ohio River and soon found another pilot. On this short excursion the *Natchez* met with a smaller boat containing the deputation sent from Tennessee to invite Lafayette to ascend the Cumberland River into Nashville. Once they were told that Lafayette was expected in St. Louis it was determined that part of the delegates would remain aboard the steamboat *Mechanic* and the rest would go along to St. Louis. "We left the *beautiful,* to enter the *great* river," wrote Levasseur about the reentry into the Mississippi.

The *Natchez* was now coming into a more settled area of the West. The lands were elevated and there were more houses on the river banks. Traces of old French buildings were visible and beautiful islands interrupted the monotony of the river. The boat passed the village of Herculaneum, which had been formed around a bullet factory built upon rock.

After nine days aboard the *Natchez,* the travelers sighted the tiny village that had once been called "Empty Pocket," but whose name had been changed to Carondelet. Although it was only a few miles from St. Louis, there was no chance of arriving in the capital by daylight, so the travelers passed the night at anchor and many villagers boarded the boat to bring gifts to Lafayette. He accepted

62. Triumphal arch built in St. Louis for Lafayette's visit in 1825. *Courtesy American Antiquarian Society*

63. Pierre Chouteau house, where Lafayette was entertained while in St. Louis. *From an etching by Pierre Chouteau, Missouri Historical Society*

geese, a young fawn, rocks, minerals, and shells as graciously as he had accepted more valuable gifts from the prosperous eastern cities.

On the morning of April 29 Governor Clark of Missouri and Governor Coles of Illinois boarded the *Natchez* to escort Lafayette into St. Louis. A few minutes later another steamboat, crowded with St. Louis citizens, pulled alongside and the people saluted the nation's guest with three loud cheers. Accompanying Lafayette in the elegant calash provided for him was Augustus Choteau, founder of St. Louis. After welcoming ceremonies Lafayette was taken to the house of Mr. Choteau's son, which was thrown open to all citizens without distinction who wanted to greet Lafayette. Dinner was served at the Choteau home.

The citizens of St. Louis had been advised in advance that Lafayette could spend only a few hours as their guest and they packed as much into that time as possible. Lafayette was taken on a tour of the city, visited Indian monuments, saw a collection of Indian relics owned by the governor, and was presented with an Indian garment made of buffalo skin.

In the evening a ball was held that was called "the most brilliant social event that had ever been seen upon the western shore of the Mississippi." Levasseur noted that "the splendid decorations of the room and the beauty of the ladies made us completely forget that we were on the confines of a wilderness which the savages themselves consider as insufficient for the supply of simple wants, since they only frequent it occasionally." Lafayette left the ball at midnight to get some needed rest before the boat weighed anchor in the morning.

18

SHIPWRECK ON THE OHIO RIVER

Governor Coles, of Illinois, was with Lafayette on the *Natchez* when it steamed away from St. Louis on Saturday morning, April 30. Lafayette had not yet visited this state and the governor had prevailed upon the General to stop in the small town of Kaskeskia, eighty miles downriver. The steamboat arrived at the village at one in the afternoon, and since the people had not been advised of a possible visit from Lafayette nothing had been prepared.

As soon as word spread that the *Natchez* was approaching and would stop, someone was dispatched for a carriage and the citizens of the town were gathered minutes after Lafayette landed. An escort was quickly formed and the procession marched to the house of General Edgar, a soldier of the Revolution, who opened his home for a public reception. This visit gave Governor Coles an opportunity to welcome Lafayette officially in behalf of the people of Illinois, and while the speeches were being made the women of Kaskeskia managed to prepare a banquet. This was followed by an impromptu ball, which lasted until midnight.

Before nightfall on the following day the *Natchez* reached the mouth of the Ohio River, where the *Mechanic* waited with part of the Tennessee delegation, and the passengers left the comfort of the Mississippi riverboat for the less commodious, narrow boat built to navigate the shallow waters of the Cumberland River.

The *Mechanic* entered the Cumberland at eight o'clock on the evening of May 2 and after daybreak there were many stops along

151

the river to allow people who had come down to its banks to board and pay respects to Lafayette. As a result, progress up the river was slow.

On Wednesday, May 4, the banks of the river became elevated and around eight in the morning bells were heard in the distance. This was a signal to people of Nashville that the *Mechanic* had been sighted and last-minute plans were made to give Lafayette a hero's welcome in Nashville. Tennessee's own hero, Andrew Jackson, received Lafayette and rode in his carriage in the procession into the city. On entering Nashville the parade marched under a triumphal arch on the summit of which was inscribed "Welcome Lafayette, the Friend of the United States." Above this floated the American flag attached to a lance surmounted by a liberty cap. The public square was decorated with thousands of flags and an elevated platform built under another great arch. It was here that Lafayette was formally received by the governor of Tennessee.

After Lafayette answered the welcoming speeches forty old and enfeebled Revolutionary veterans, many of them mutilated in the war, advanced as best they could from either side of the arch and showered affection and words of praise on Lafayette. The old men had been brought from all areas of the state and one, especially, captured the hearts of the crowd when he embraced Lafayette and cried, "I have enjoyed two happy days in my life; that when I landed with you at Charleston in 1777; and the present. Now that I have seen you once again, I have nothing more to wish for; I have lived long enough."

In the late afternoon a public dinner was held for over two hundred citizens and presided over by Andrew Jackson. Following the final toast the party departed for the Masonic Lodge, where Lafayette was received with full honors by three hundred brothers. Another banquet followed, and upon returning home to quarters Lafayette found the entire city illuminated and many houses and stores decorated with transparencies representing his portrait and patriotic symbols.

The next day Lafayette reviewed the Tennessee militia and breakfast was served under a tent. The next stops were at Nashville Academy and Cumberland College. At ceremonies at the college two new chairs were announced in honor of Lafayette and Andrew Jackson for the teaching of languages and philosophy.

At one o'clock Lafayette was at the Hermitage, the home of Andrew and Rachel Jackson. Mrs. Jackson had invited many of the neighboring farmers and their families to meet the famous visitor. Jackson showed Lafayette, George, and Auguste his garden and farm buildings, which were neat and orderly, but the presence of slaves on the property were again a source of consternation to the guests.

Upon returning to the house, Jackson, at the insistence of some of his guests, showed them the arms that had been presented to him in honor of his achievements on the battlefield. These were a sword presented by Congress, a saber given him by the Army for his achievements at the battle of New Orleans, and a pair of pistols that Lafayette had presented to Washington in 1778. Lafayette expressed his delight at finding the pistols in the hands of so worthy a soldier, although it was never explained to him how Jackson happened to have them. "I believe myself worthy of them," said Jackson, "if not from what I have done, at least for what I wished to do for my country." There is some evidence that he then presented the pistols to Lafayette. Dinner was given Lafayette at the Hermitage and a brilliant ball was held in Nashville in the evening.

Early the folowing morning the *Mechanic* descended the Cumberland River and the next day entered the Ohio and arrived at dawn on the following day on the shore opposite Shawneetown, where Lafayette attended a dinner and then boarded the boat to ascend the Ohio River. There were a number of passengers aboard besides the General, his valet, George, and Auguste. Deputations had come along from the states of Missouri, Tennessee, and Kentucky, and private citizens had asked permission to accompany

Lafayette to Louisville. There was not an empty bed in the great cabin that all passengers shared. Exceptions were Lafayette, George, Levasseur, and a Mr. de Syon, a friend of the three, who had been on the journey throughout the southern and western tours since Washington. These four shared the "ladies cabin," in the stern of the vessel.

Evidently, the United States mail had little trouble reaching the frontier in 1825, for Levasseur and Lafayette spent all of May 8 answering the huge amount of letters that had reached them from all parts of the country. Lafayette also spent part of the day dictating some directions for changes and improvements at La Grange so that his farm superintendent could implement these orders before his employer returned to France. Tired from a full day's labor, Lafayette was in bed and asleep before ten o'clock. George had been on deck and when he returned to the cabin he remarked that it was so dark a night it was remarkable that the pilot could navigate the boat. Then he also went to bed and Levasseur remained awake to converse with Mr. de Syon and to correct some notes that he had made during the day's dictation. By eleven o'clock only these two men, two sailors, and the pilot were still awake.

At midnight the vessel suddenly received a violent jolt and stopped short. Lafayette awoke and George sprang from his bed. Levasseur, who was still dressed, ran up on deck to see what had happened and there he met two fellow passengers who had come up from the men's cabin to find the cause of the trouble. They told Levasseur that the boat probably had struck a sand bar and that there was no great danger. Levasseur next went to the great cabin, where he found some commotion, but the majority of the passengers had not even left their beds. Not trusting the opinions of others, Levasseur then seized a light and ran forward on the boat, arriving at the same time as the captain. Together they went forward only to find that the hold was already filled with water, which was rushing in torrents through a large hole in the hull.

The captain's first thought was for his illustrious passenger and he directed Lavasseur to bring Lafayette to his lifeboat. Levasseur ran to his cabin and found Lafayette, who by this time was permitting his servant to dress him. The General asked "What news?" and was told by his secretary, "We shall go to the bottom, General, if we cannot extricate ourselves, and we have not a moment to spare."

Levasseur then began to collect all papers that he could find and threw them into his portfolio. George quickly gathered some objects that he thought would be necessary to his father's comfort. Lafayette had not yet finished dressing and he begged the others to go ahead of him to arrange for their own escape. George refused, saying, "What! Do you think that in these circumstances we would leave you for a moment?" Levasseur grabbed one of Lafayette's hands and George the other and they dragged the old General to the door. Halfway up the stairs Lafayette remembered that he had forgotten his snuffbox ornamented with a picture of Washington and wanted to return for it. Levasseur ran back to the cabin, found the box, and soon caught up with the others.

By this time the vessel was rolling violently and the other passengers were rushing around on deck and screaming. Levasseur was certain that the boat would sink before they had time to escape, but at last they reached the deck. Later, Levasseur recalled the people were crying out for Lafayette as if they would not think to save themselves until they were certain that the hero was safely off the boat.

It was so dark that no one could see Lafayette anyway, and the boat had heeled to starboard so much that it was difficult to keep one's footing. With the help of two sailors the captain had brought his small boat alongside the *Mechanic* and shouted for Lafayette. Levasseur pushed the General toward the sound and he was shoved into the lifeboat. This was no easy task. Levasseur jumped into the boat first and realized that precautions would have to be taken if Lafayette were not to end up in the water. The steamboat was rocking violently and the small boat was four feet below deck. Levasseur steadied the boat, the captain grabbed the edge to help hold the boat steady, and two persons, taking Lafayette by the shoulders, lowered him toward the lifeboat, where Levasseur caught him. The weight of the falling man threw Auguste down and the boat almost capsized.

The lifeboat then was pushed off as rapidly as possible to keep other passengers from boarding and overloading it. The captain had come along and navigated the boat toward shore in the pitch black of the night. Two sailors did the rowing. In all, there were nine passengers aboard, including a seven-year-old child, and when noses were counted Lafayette became alarmed that George was not included. He became hysterical and called for his son over and over, but his voice was drowned out by the cries of the passengers and crew still aboard the *Mechanic* and the noise of the vessel itself as steam escaped from its engine.

Auguste attempted to comfort Lafayette by assuring him that George was a good swimmer, but this had no effect, and as Lafayette paced up and down calling "George! George!" Levasseur and the captain jumped back into the boat to begin rescuing more passengers. At this point the steamboat was still floating but was on her beam ends, and the next boatload of a dozen people was brought to shore. Levasseur dreaded having to tell his employer that he had neither seen nor spoken to George, de Syon, or Bastien.

As Auguste and the captain emptied the boat of its second load of survivors and prepared to return for others there was a great noise and many loud screams and it became obvious that the *Mechanic* was sinking. Swimmers began to arrive on shore, but George Lafayette was not among them. When the lifeboat returned from its third trip, this time without Levasseur, who had remained on shore to comfort his distraught employer, those on shore were informed that the *Mechanic* had not sunk entirely, but that the starboard side was under water.

Levasseur went again into the lifeboat and was rowed to the wreck. He called loudly for George, but received no answer. He did spot Bastien, who was holding onto the roof of the upper cabin. The servant slid down and fortunately fell into the lifeboat. Levasseur was then rowed around to the stern, and when he called for George this time finally got an answer. George's voice was perfectly calm. "Are you in safety?" Auguste asked. George replied, "I could not be better."

On this trip everything from Lafayette's cabin that could be salvaged was put into the lifeboat. These were a small suitcase belonging to George, a suitcase belonging to his father, and a portmanteau in which Levasseur had put the two hundred letters he had written the day before. Everything else was lost and later Lafayette was to write to a friend in Philadelphia, "This loss throws all my correspondence into confusion. I have not saved a single memorandum."

When Auguste was rowed to shore he hastened to assure the distraught General that his son was safe. The vessel could not sink any more and, knowing there was nothing more he could do in his lifesaving efforts, Levasseur occupied himself in attempting to make his employer more comfortable. While he was gathering wood for a fire, George and the remaining passengers arrived.

Everyone was safe and accounted for and huge fires kept the passengers warm through the night. Lafayette was bedded down on a mattress that had floated in from the wreck and that was almost completely dry on one side. Many of the passengers and crew kept busy through the night gathering wood for the fires, but, to add to the discomforts, it began to rain.

At daybreak some of the sailors took trips out to the wreck to salvage whatever they could in the way of food and to search for whatever baggage that was salvagable. A trunk belonging to Lafayette was brought to shore along with a leg of smoked venison, some bisquits, a keg of claret, and a keg of madeira. Later, Auguste Levasseur described the picture on shore that morning as "interesting." The river bank was covered with wrecks of all kinds and many persons wandered around searching for objects that belonged to them. Some bemoaned the extent of their losses, while others laughed at the various states of undress in which they found themselves.

Lafayette was persuaded to get into the lifeboat once more to be rowed across the river to a house that had been sighted, but as the small boat pulled away two steamboats were seen descending the river and, by luck, the owner of one of the boats, a Mr. Neilson, was one of the shipwrecked passengers. Neilson ordered the *Paragon,* coming from Louisville and heading toward New Orleans with a load of whiskey and tobacco, to be put at the disposal of the Tennessee Committee and to transport Lafayette on the remainder of his voyage.

Everyone except Captain Hall of the *Mechanic* boarded the rescue vesel. The captain decided to remain with the *Mechanic* in the hope of salvaging something from it. He had lost twelve hundred dollars in the wreck as well as other goods and the ship itself. Nevertheless, he was more depressed at having endangered the life of the nation's guest, and in order to comfort the dejected man, the passengers drew up and signed a declaration in which they attested that the loss of the *Mechanic* could not be attributed to either the ineptness or imprudence of Captain Hall and that he had shown great courage during the tragedy. This document did not entirely console him.

Two days later, on May 11, the *Paragon* stopped at Portland, three miles below Louisville. The shipwreck had taken place about one hundred and thirty-five miles from that city, near the mouth of Deer Creek.

It continued to rain through the two-day Lafayette celebration in Louisville and Mr. Neilson, the owner of the *Paragon,* was fêted as a hero along with Lafayette. The city presented a silver trophy to the steamboat owner on which was engraved the appreciation of the citizens of Tennessee and Kentucky for the generous manner in which he had risked a part of his fortune so that Lafayette should not be further delayed or inconvenienced. It was noted that Mr. Neilson's insurance company decided not to charge extra for the valuable passengers that the boat had taken aboard.

Despite the bad weather Lafayette crossed the river the next day to be a guest of Jeffersonville, Indiana. The barbecue of a bear was cancelled because of the rain and an indoor banquet held instead. In the evening Lafayette returned to Louisville for a gala performance in the theater and a ball.

19

JOURNEY TO
NIAGARA FALLS AND THE
NEW ERIE CANAL

The next leg of Lafayette's tour was, fortunately, overland, and would take him across Kentucky and into Ohio, where a celebration was being planned in Cincinnati. He left Louisville on Friday, May 13, and at the end of the day arrived in Shelbyville. After a reception and banquet and night's sleep Lafayette and his companions, escorted by a troop of Lafayette Cavalry, again took to the road and at four in the afternoon reached Frankfort, then the capital of Kentucky. In Frankfort a large public dinner with places for eight hundred people was served in the town square. The next day Lafayette passed through Versailles and stayed the night at a mansion five miles outside Lexington.

On Monday a group of cavalry from Lafayette County escorted the nation's guest into Lexington. It was raining again, but when the procession was formed artillery discharged to announce to the citizens of Lexington that the parade was about to start and the rain stopped as if by magic. An advertisement in the *Lexington Reporter* for that day read as follows:

Just received at the bookstore of Henry H. Hunt, Main Street, Cockades like those mounted by the Republicans during the Revolutionary War and worn by citizens in the Eastern Cities during the visit of the "Nation's Guest."

160

Welcoming ceremonies over, Lafayette then visited the University of Transylvania, where the students eulogized their guest in Latin, French, and English. At Lexington Female Academy the General was entertained by a chorus of one hundred and fifty voices rendering original patriotic songs, and he heard speeches and original poems extolling his virtues. Lafayette was not the least jaded or bored by this sort of ceremony, and Levasseur noted, "At last he tore himself from a scene of emotion too violent to be supported for any length of time."

During this visit Lafayette made a side trip to Ashland, the home of Henry Clay. Clay was in Washington, but Lafayette spent some time with his wife and children. The next day he sat for the artist Jouett and later breakfasted with the Masonic brethren of Lexington. A great cake baked in his honor was displayed in the city. In the next town he visited, Blue Springs, a giant cheese, weighing five hundred pounds, was a major tribute to the hero.

On the nineteenth of May at ten o'clock a deputation from Cincinnati waited on boats moored on the left bank of the Ohio River, across from the city, to meet Lafayette's entourage. Lafayette and his escorts boarded the largest of these boats and crossed to Cincinnati. Along with the usual festivities there was a display that night of fireworks at the Globe Inn and at daybreak on Friday six hundred schoolchildren assembled outside of Lafayette's lodgings to sing a welcoming song, after which Lafayette reviewed the militia and saw a representative procession of all the trades of the city pass in review. In the parade, mounted on wheels and decorated with flags, was the state barge, in which Lafayette had crossed the Ohio River the day before. Escorting the barge were those veterans of the Revolution who could still manage to march.

In the afternoon Lafayette was visited by the Swiss Society of Cincinnati, all of whom lived in a community called Vevey, outside the city. They were engaged in attempting to establish a wine industry in Ohio and they brought samples of their product for Lafayette to taste. They hoped, as did many other manufacturers, craftsmen, and farmers, for an "endorsement" by the French visitor. Lafayette had retired to rest up for the evening's festivities when the Swiss wine producers arrived, and George and Auguste were obliged to sample their product. It was later described by Levasseur as "by no means exquisite."

More than five hundred persons attended the ball given that evening for the nation's guest and many distinguished persons traveled great distances to be there. Lafayette called Cincinnati the "eighth wonder of the world" and marveled at its rapid growth and prosperity. He had another reason for having warm feelings toward the state of Ohio. Its constitution guaranteed freedom to every slave who stepped across its borders.

At midnight Lafayette embarked on the steamboat *Herald* to travel three hundred miles to Wheeling and stops were made in Portsmouth, Gallipolis, and Marietta. Festivities were held at all towns and from Wheeling Lafayette was escorted to Washington, Pennsylvania, and then passed through Brownsville and arrived at Uniontown in Fayette County.

On Sunday the travelers continued on to Elizabeth for a noontime banquet, after which they boarded a boat and descended the Monongahela River to Braddock's Field. On the old battlefield had been built a mansion belonging to George Wallace, and it was here that Lafayette was met by the Pittsburgh delegation.

The road to Pittsburgh, through Lawrenceville and Allegheny Arsenal, was lined with people, and the procession advanced slowly toward the city. Pittsburgh's reception of Lafayette was brilliant and the major events were a banquet and the presentation of the schoolchildren. Although his schedule was a busy one Lafayette requested time to inspect some of the factories of the town, which he said compared with those of St. Etienne, France, or Manchester, England. "He was struck," Levasseur wrote later, "by the excellence and perfection of the processes employed in the various workshops which he examined; but that which interested him above all was the manufacture of glass, some patterns of which were presented to him, that, for their clearness and transparency, might have been admired even by the side of the glass of Baccarat."

His visit to Pittsburgh over, Lafayette and his escort of militia next went to Butler and spent the night of June 1 at Mercer. In the morning he visited Meadville and Allegheny College and reached Waterford by nightfall. His next major destination was Erie, New York, where he arrived on Friday, June 3.

In Erie there was much celebration and some discussion of the War of 1812 and the exploits of the local hero, Admiral Perry. Captured English flags and sails from the naval battles of the war were used as decoration in the banquet hall, and when this event was over Lafayette left by carriage to ride up to Dunkirk, where a steamboat waited to conduct him to Buffalo. The distance of fifty miles was covered by traveling all night without stopping, and the villagers along the route lit huge bonfires and waited through the night hoping to catch a glimpse of Lafayette's carriage.

At one point during the carriage ride to Dunkirk the passengers were jolted awake by the sound of artillery and, looking out, saw thousands of small lights suspended from surrounding trees and houses. Lafayette alighted and found himself in the midst of an avenue formed by men and boys on one side and women and girls on the other. Although he had been sound asleep moments before he was so touched by this tribute that he walked down the rows of people and shook hands with everyone. The entire population of Fredonia, New York, had waited all through the chilly night to greet the nation's guest. They conducted him to a large platform, lighted by barrels of burning rosin, which had been built in the center of the town, and where the mayor and a reception committee waited to greet the tired hero. At Lafayette's request, the ceremonies were "abridged" because of the coolness of the evening and the necessity to get tired children to bed.

When Lafayette arrived at Buffalo the next afternoon he went through the usual welcoming ceremonies and was then taken to the Eagle Tavern to rest. However, many people waited there to be presented to him and among this group was an old Indian named Red Jacket, a chief of the Seneca tribe. He reminded Lafayette that they had met in 1784 at Fort Schuyler. The General asked the Indian, who was "much broken by time and intemperance," the whereabouts of a young Indian who had strongly opposed peace at that conference.

"He is before you," replied Red Jacket.

"Time has much changed us," Lafayette said, "for then we were young and active."

"Ah," answered the old Indian, "time has been less severe on you than me. He has left you a fresh countenence, and a head well covered with hair, whilst as for me—look!" He removed the kerchief that covered his head. "Look!" he said. The Indian's head was completely bald.

The crowd observing this scene roared with laughter. Everyone in America, with the exclusion of Red Jacket, knew that Lafayette's copious head of reddish brown hair was a wig.

The next morning, after a night of festivities in Buffalo, Lafayette and his party set out in carriages for Niagara Falls. They stopped at Black Rock for breakfast and then continued the journey. "A few hours later," recorded Levasseur, "a hollow rumbling which seemed to shake the earth and a thick column of vapor which we saw at a distance rising towards the clouds made it clear that we were about to see one of the greatest wonders of nature." The day at the Falls included a public dinner and a trip over a precipitous bridge to Goat Island, where legends of the powers of the falls were told.

The night was spent in Lewiston and the following day Lafayette was a guest at Fort Niagara, where he was served breakfast by the officers' wives. The General then proceeded to Lockport, which, instead of the usual artillery fire, greeted the hero with a loud explosion different from any that he had previously heard. Hundreds of small charges, used for blasting rock during the building of the Erie Canal, had been placed in strategic spots and were set off as Lafayette entered the town. This explosion hurled fragments of rock into the air, and miraculously, there were no accidents.

Lockport was a new town built to accommodate workers on the canal. Levasseur wrote, "The appearance of Lockport filled us with astonishment and admiration. In every part may be heard the sound of the hatchet and hammer. The trees are felled, fashioned under the hands of the carpenter, and raised on the same spot in the form of a house." A huge hotel already had been built to accommodate new settlers, and while there were not yet many of the necessities of life, Lafayette was amazed to learn that a newspaper had been established.

After ceremonies at Lockport, conducted by Stephen Van Rensselaer, president of the Board of Canal Commisioners, under a triumphal arch built of green branches, and other festivities, Lafayette boarded a canal boat that would take him to Rochester. On the way to the boat he inspected locks that had been cut from solid rock to a depth of twenty-five feet, and as a parting gift he was presented a box of rock specimens representing the variety of formations through which the canal had been cut.

The barge *Rochester* was comfortable and convenient, and in the early morning, while the travelers were still in their cabin, they heard the name of Lafayette being called. They went on deck and found that the boat appeared to be suspended in the air. On both sides of the canal were huge crowds. The barge had reached a point where the canal crossed the Genesee River and an aquaduct had been built that was four hundred yards long. The engineering feat was explained to Levasseur, who said, "This kind of construction appears familiar to the Americans. The bridges are usually of an elegance and boldness of execution that is inconceivable."

Lafayette received a great welcome in the city of Rochester and left there on the afternoon of June 7 for Canandaigua, where he spent the night. He went through Geneva, Auburn, and Waterloo as well as other small villages along the route to Syracuse. He made the trip of one hundred and fifty miles as rapidly as he could and

64. Platter with four-portrait border showing Lafayette with Jefferson, Clinton, and Washington. Center scene is of Faulkborn Hall, in England, but vignette in lower border is scene of entrance of Erie Canal into the Hudson, at Albany. Made by Stevenson, Staffordshire, England, around 1825. *Mattatuck Museum*

relays of horses and drivers were provided along the way. Although the citizens of Syracuse had expected the hero the night before he finally arrived, the sumptuous banquet they had prepared became a splendid early breakfast and after a procession Lafayette left aboard a canal boat by nine o'clock in the morning.

Always mindful of his pledge to the people of Boston, the General determined to travel day and night and stopped only briefly in the small towns along the canal system. He stayed overnight in Rome, however, and attended a quick reception in Utica. He was obliged to refuse the honor of laying the cornerstone to a monument in memory of Baron von Steuben and after only three hours in Utica he boarded the packet boat *Governor Clinton* to descend the canal. The vessel, drawn by white horses, was pelted with flowers as it passed under bridges on which children with filled baskets had been strategically placed.

The following day Lafayette attended a reception in his honor at Little Falls and reached Schenectady at eight in the evening. The citizens of this town crammed three-days' entertainment into three hours, after which Lafayette set out by carriage for Cruttenden's Hotel, in Albany, where he spent a quiet Sunday and took time to write a letter to Mayor Quincy of Boston to inform him that he was on his way to redeem his "sacred and most cordial pledge" to be in Boston on the fifteenth.

20

CELEBRATION OF THE ANNIVERSARY OF THE BATTLE OF BUNKER HILL

Although Lafayette still had some distance to travel before reaching Boston, he stopped in Pittsfield, Massachusetts, for a few hours on Monday, June 13. He knew that the roads would be good for the rest of his trip and by this time was less anxious that his schedule would be disturbed. He spent a night in Worthington, Massachusetts, and the next day proceeded through Chesterfield and Northampton and went on to Belchertown and Worcester.

Lafayette entered the city of Boston around noon on the fifteenth of June. As Bostonians had followed reports of his amazing tour of the country there had been much speculation and doubt concerning his ability to reach their city in time for the celebration, and many considered it almost a miracle that he was able to fulfill his promise. In less than four months Lafayette had traveled a distance of close to five thousand miles. Luck and careful planning played a part in his accomplishment. In addition, Lafayette and his companions had been privy to help along the route that would not have been available to less venerated men.

The skeptical citizens of Boston should have had more faith, for they certainly had had plenty of reassurance from Lafayette that he planned to make good his pledge. In many of his letters to friends of the city he often told them that the commitment was uppermost in his mind throughout his long tour through the South

65. Militia snare drum made in Pittsfield, Massachusetts, in 1824, in honor of Lafayette's visit. Brown tarnished bentwood shell secured with brass-headed tacks. *Courtesy Old Sturbridge Village*

66. Detail of painted decoration on drum. Red-and-gilt eight-pointed star around breather hole and stylized sunburst above with four ribbon motifs on sides. *Courtesy Old Sturbridge Village*

67. Label on drum reads, "ABNER STEVENS/Keeps constantly on hand for sale/at his/MUSIC SHOP AND STORE/ in Pittsfield, Mass./ Bass and Tenour/ DRUMS, FIFES/and most kinds of/ MUSICAL INSTRU-MENTS, STRINGS, REEDS, BOWS, &c. &c./Made in the neatest manner and sold for Cheap Cash/ 1824." *Courtesy Old Sturbridge Village*

and West. His letter to Mayor Quincy, dated June 12, was one of the most recent:

Thus far I am come to redeem my sacred and most cordial pledge. We shall reach Boston on the 15th. I will tell you, between us, that I have been informed the legislature intend to receive my personal respects, in which case it becomes proper for me to be arrived two days before the Bunker Hill ceremony. As to what I am to do, I cannot do better than to refer myself to your friendly advice,—and shall hastily offer you and your family my most affectionate grateful respects.

A description of what went on in the Quincy household once this letter was received was recorded by the mayor's daughter in her diary:

[My] father was immediately obliged although it was midnight to rise and go out in order to give it [the letter] to the printers and have it published in the papers of the next morning.

About three o'clock in the afternoon information came that General Lafayette had arrived at Mr. Lloyd's who had invited him to stay at his house during his visit to the city. We concluded the General would be too much fatigued to think of paying visits today, so we quietly went to repose ourselves, as we felt tired after the disturbance last night, and seeing company all the morning, but another express soon thundered at the door to say that General Lafayette would be at our house in twenty minutes. We all returned to the parlour and prepared for the reception of the General and at the appointed time he arrived, attended by his son, M. Levasseur, and Mr. Lloyd. Lafayette and the gentlemen of his party shook hands with us most cordially and really seemed highly delighted to see us again. They said we could not imagine how much pleasure they felt when they once more came in sight of Boston, that it seemed to them almost as if they were arriving at home.

Although one might have thought that the arduous journey since Lafayette's last visit in Boston would have taken its toll, Miss Quincy reported otherwise:

The General really looks younger than he did when he was here last Autumn and both he and his attendants have improved both in health and appearance by their tour through the United States. When we spoke of the remarkable expedition with which they had accomplished their journey, they replied; Oh there is nothing surprising in that:—when people have carriages, horses, boats, all of them in first order, prepared for them and awaiting them at every step as we have had, they do not deserve any credit for travelling fast.

On the following day, according to plans previously made, Lafayette went to the capitol, where he was greeted by the new governor of Massachusetts, Mr. Lincoln, who, along with representatives of other governing bodies, congratulated Lafayette on the happy termination of his long journey. Miss Quincy, in the gallery with other Boston ladies, wrote, "It was interesting to hear La Fayette speak in public in reply to the Governor's address. Considering his age and foreign accent he spoke very well and could be distinctly heard."

Meanwhile, all of Boston had been preparing for the ceremonies that were to take place the next day. Boston, being more fortunate than many of the other cities that had played host to Lafayette, had beautiful weather on June 17, 1825, and at dawn the roar of cannon woke the citizens of the city as they had done fifty years previously.

The procession to Bunker Hill was composed of seven thousand persons who formed a line of march at ten-thirty. At the head were two hundred officers and soldiers of the Revolution, followed by forty veterans, who were all that remained of those who had fought at the battle of Bunker Hill. Mercifully, these old men were transported in open carriages decorated with large ribbons on which was inscribed "June 17th, 1775." Behind them marched a long array of subscribers to the monument, formed in ranks of six abreast. Then followed two thousand Masons dressed in the ornaments and symbols of their order.

Lafayette's position in the parade was next and he had been provided with a "superb calash drawn by six white horses." In the

68. *Right.* Coach used by Lafayette in procession celebrating laying of cornerstone of Bunker Hill Monument. *Photograph courtesy of State Street Bank and Trust Company, Boston*

69. *Below.* Rare print of Lafayette, dressed in classical style and officiating at laying of cornerstone of Bunker Hill Monument. Print, first published in 1906, is from original lithograph by Langlume, after a drawing by Mlle. d'Herirlly, Paris. *Photograph courtesy of State Street Bank and Trust Company, Boston*

BUNKER HILL MONUMENT ASSOCIA-TION.

Corrected Order of Procession, for the Seventeenth of June, 1825.

The Procession will move from the State House PRECISELY at TEN o'clock, through Park, Common, and School streets, Cornhill, Dock square, Union, Hanover, and Prince streets, over Charles River Bridge, the Main street, Green and High streets, to the site of the Monument.

Those who constitute the Procession, are respectfully requested to assemble at the places for them, hereinafter respectively designated, *precisely* at NINE o'clock, that the procession may be arranged in season to move *punctually* at the appointed hour.

For obvious reasons, (which the good sense of the public will duly appreciate) NO CARRIAGES, *but from necessity*, will move in the procession.

MILITARY ESCORT.

SURVIVORS OF THE BATTLE, with badges:—Bunker Hill, June 17, 1775. To assemble precisely at 9 o'clock, at the Subscription House, corner of Park and Beacon streets, where they will receive their badges, and be placed in open carriages, to form part of the procession.

THE MEMBERS OF THE BUNKER HILL MONUMENT ASSOCIATION, distinguished by badges worn on the left breast; every member who walks in the procession will wear the badge, "B H M A." Members are to assemble in the Beacon street Mall.

THE GRAND LODGE OF MASSACHUSETTS :—The Most Worshipful Grand Master, John Abbot, Esq. having accepted an invitation to lay the Corner-Stone; accompanied by the Fraternity of Masons. To assemble in the Mall by Common street.

The President of B. H. M. A.

The Rev. Joseph Thaxter, Revolutionary Chaplain, and the Rev. James Walker.

Chaplains of the occasion.

Vice Presidents of B. H. M. A.

Directors.

Committee of Correspondence.

Other Committees.

Secretary and Treasurer.

To assemble at the office of B. H. M. A.

THE PRESIDENT OF THE UNITED STATES, in a carriage.

(It is regretted that the President is unable to attend.)

General LAFAYETTE, and Son, in an open carriage.

Gen. Lafayette's Suite, in a carriage.

THE OFFICERS OF THE REVOLUTIONARY ARMY AND REVOLUTIONARY NAVY. To assemble at the Adjutant General's Office, State House, where they will be furnished with badges.

THE CINCINNATI OF MASSACHUSETTS, and of *other* States. To assemble in the West Entry (lower floor) of the State House.

His Excellency the GOVERNOR.

His Honour the LIEUT. GOVERNOR and the EXECUTIVE COUNCIL.

Adjutant General, Secretary, Treasurer.

The Honourable the Senate.

The Honourable House of Representatives.

Governors of other States in the Union.

On the westwardly side of the area of the State House floor.

Heads of Department of United States. At the same place as next above.

Senators of the United States. At same place as next above.

Members of the House of Representatives of the United States. At same place as next above.

Members of Foreign Legations, and Consuls. At same place.

Judges of the United States Courts, and of the State Courts of Massachusetts and other States.

Attorney and Solicitor General, Attorney of U. States, Marshal of U. S. Sheriffs, Clerks. On the floor of the State House.

Delegations from Charleston, S. C. and Providence, R. I. specially commissioned to attend this celebration. On the area of the State House.

Strangers of distinction, of other States, invited to attend. Area of floor of State House.

Officers of the Army and Navy of the U. States. State House floor.

Members of the Legislatures of other States.—State House floor.

The Mayor of the City of Boston, President of the Common Council, and Board of Aldermen of the City of Boston, and the Chairman and Selectmen of Charlestown. State House floor.

PRESIDENTS and OFFICERS OF COLLEGES, and the Reverend CLERGY. To assemble at Mrs Torrey's, late Gov. Hancock's house, Beacon st.

HEADS OF SOCIETIES. In Eastern Entry of the State House.

The HISTORICAL SOCIETY of Massachusetts. In the Treasurer's Office, State House.

Delegation of the PILGRIM SOCIETY (of Plymouth.) As next above.

OFFICERS of the MILITIA, in uniform. To assemble and form on the west side of the State House Yard, extending along the west end of the State House, and in the rear thereof.

INVITED CITIZENS of Massachusetts. At the Land Office, State House.

The celebration intended, will consist of the procession in the order before stated. On arriving at the site of the monument, the different parts of the procession will be distributed, in close order, on the sides of the square, into which no persons can be admitted, *the space being limited*, but those who belong to the procession.

The ceremonies of laying the Corner Stone, will then take place, and immediately afterwards the procession will be disposed of in the Amphitheatre, erected on the north side of the hill, to hear the ADDRESS, to be there delivered by the *President of the Association*, accompanied by suitable solemnities.

A new procession will then be formed, to be composed of those persons *only*, who shall have provided themselves with cards of admission to the dinner, and of the few persons, whom the Directors supposed they should consult the wishes of the Association in receiving as GUESTS, and, so formed, this procession will move to the place prepared on Bunker Hill to dine.

A part of the Amphitheatre (all that could be) has been appropriated for LADIES, who will enter by ONE Avenue on Elm street. The streets leading to the Hill, where the ceremonies are to take place will, with a view to prevent accidents and calamities, BE ABSOLUTELY BARRED AGAINST CARRIAGES. Gentlemen who attend Ladies, *will not be admitted into the Amphitheatre.* Ladies will be received from their attendants, at the entrance to the Avenue, by Marshals appointed for that purpose. When the procession has left the hill, gentlemen will be admitted to attend ladies thence, and not before. The ladies will remain seated until the procession moves to dinner. The avenue for *Ladies* will be open precisely at ELEVEN o'clock.

As there will be in this assembly many persons of *far advanced age*, and who are consequently *infirm*, all the ceremonies will be as SHORT as can be, consistently with the dignity of the occasion. This consideration will have its due weight in impressing all concerned with the necessity of PUNCTUALITY and READINESS that no time may be wasted.

It having been stated that the government of the association had assumed the payment of the expenses of SURVIVORS in attending, on this occasion, it should be known, *that it is not so.* No authority to do this, nor to incur any expense not absolutely necessary, has been given, or exercised. If any such payment be made, it must be a consequence of an expressed opinion, of the members of the Association.

WM. SULLIVAN,
SETH KNOWLES,
SAM'L D. HARRIS, } *Executive Committee of B. H. M. A.*

Boston, June 15, 1825.

carriages immediately following were his son, Levasseur, the governor of Massachusetts and his staff, and many persons of distinction. Militia and a large martial band, made up of musicians from the entire country, followed. Discharges of artillery, fired at regular intervals along the route, drowned out the music and the enthusiastic cheering of thousands of spectators.

At twelve-thirty the procession arrived at the site of the proposed monument. The modest wooden pyramid that had previously covered the site had been removed. Miss Quincy, who had gone to Bunker Hill ahead of the procession, described in her diary the ascension of the long parade:

At length the report of cannon and the sound of military music announced the approach of the procession and the Infantry appeared at a distance on the brow of the hill, advancing to the music of one of our favorite national airs. The military escort crossed the hill in a line, towards the place where the cornerstone of the Monument was to be laid, followed by a great multitude of Free Masons in their singular dresses and bearing splendid banners and then came the rest of the procession. The cornerstone was laid on the other side of the hill, from the spot where we were stationed, we could not therefore see the ceremony, but we saw the multitude and heard the strains of soft music (a dirge to the memory of the departed) which floated towards us on breezes that blew over the hill.

A large excavation marked the spot where the cornerstone was to be laid and the honored guests grouped themselves around it. A variety of objects was placed in a box, and the stone, with much ceremony, laid over it. After a benediction a loud discharge of artillery pronounced this part of the ceremony over and the procession reformed and marched to a great amphitheater that had been specially constructed on the northeast corner of the hill.

All the officers and soldiers of the Revolution and the old veterans of Bunker Hill thoughtfully had been seated in the front rows and immediately behind them were two thousand women of Boston in brilliantly colored dresses. More than ten thousand persons filled the huge semicircle of benches that had been placed around

Services

ON

BUNKER HILL,

FOR

17 JUNE, 1825.

INTRODUCTORY PRAYER,

BY REV. JOSEPH THAXTER,

Chaplain of Col. Prescott's Regiment, 17 June, 1775.

HYMN,

BY REV. JOHN PIERPONT.

Tune—" *Old Hundred.*"

1 O, is not this a holy spot!
    'Tis the high place of Freedom's birth :—
God of our fathers! is it not
    The holiest spot of all the earth?

2 Quenched is thy flame on Horeb's side:
    The robber roams o'er Sinai now;
And those old men, thy seers, abide
    No more on Zion's mournful brow.

3 But on *this* hill thou, Lord, hast dwelt,
    Since round its head the war-cloud curled,
And wrapped our fathers, where they knelt
    In prayer and battle for a world.

4 Here sleeps their dust: 'tis holy ground:
    And we, the children of the brave,
From the four winds are gathered round,
    To lay our offering on their grave.

71. Leaflet distributed to those attending Bunker Hill ceremonies and giving lyrics to odes and hymns so that onlookers could sing along. *Courtesy American Antiquarian Society*

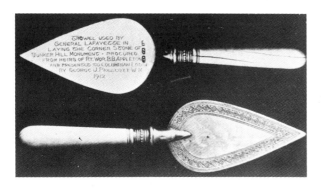

72. Trowel used by General Lafayette in laying of cornerstone of Bunker Hill Monument. *Photograph courtesy of State Street Bank and Trust Company, Boston*

the sides of the hill and thirty thousand additional spectators found room wherever they could. Although the speakers' voices were out of reach of many all maintained perfect silence through the long proceedings. On the platform, among other notables, sat Lafayette, the only surviving major-general of the Revolutionary War.

This part of the ceremonies opened with a huge chorus of voices singing a patriotic and religious ode, followed by a prayer offered by Mr. Thaxter, a veteran of the battle of Bunker Hill. The main orator was Daniel Webster, whom Levasseur described as "of lofty stature, athletic form, noble expression of face," and added, "The fire of his looks were in perfect harmony with the grandeur of the scene around." Webster, well-known for his speaking ability, outdid himself on this occasion. When he mentioned Lafayette's name, which he did frequently, all the aged veterans removed their hats and the cheers were deafening. The ceremony ended with a hymn sung by the chorus and joined in by the entire assemblage.

Luncheon was then served in an immense wooden building to four thousand invited guests while many less fortunate looked on. Before leaving the table General Lafayette rose to return his gratitude to the members of the association for erecting the monument of Bunker Hill and concluded with a toast. A great many parties took place that night in Boston, but it is probable that the one Lafayette attended was that held at the home of Mr. Webster, whose neighbor, a wealthy ship merchant, obligingly had cut a door between the two houses to make more room for the guests.

In the following days, Lafayette, accompanied by Mayor Quincy, made a farewell visit to former President Adams and there were more dinners at private homes at which the General was guest of honor. He attended a performance of *Charles II* at the Boston Theatre, into which the versatile actors managed to place a tableau of La Grange and a sentimental scene of Lafayette at the tomb of Washington. The next day Lafayette left Boston for the final portion of his American tour.

21

THROUGH NEW ENGLAND AND BACK TO NEW YORK

While Lafayette was in Boston invitations poured in requesting him not to forget his friends in the New England towns he had not yet visited. Therefore, on Tuesday, June 21, he set out once again to go to Massachusetts, New Hampshire, Maine, and Vermont. Accompanying him were the Boston Committee and a corps of volunteer cavalry. His first-day's journey took him through Charlestown, Reading, Andover, and Pembroke and he was met at the border of New Hampshire by an escort from that state. He was received the next day at the capitol by Governor Pierce and was guest of honor at a dinner for six hundred held in Concord's public square.

Lafayette, George, and Auguste traveled at a speed of eleven miles an hour through the New England states and this part of the journey was so rapid that the secretary had a difficult time keeping his detailed journal of the year's tour. "The rapidity of our movements often obliged me to forego the rigorous fulfillment of this plan," he wrote. The three often rode through so many towns and villages in one day that he could not even remember their names.

A writer who accompanied Lafayette through New Hampshire left a description of the carriage used by the General:

My equipage consisted of three carriages—a barouche, drawn by four horses, a four-horse stage coach, and a two-horse covered carriage for baggage. The barouche was precisely the thing needed for the occasion. It was of ample dimensions, the driver's seat was elevated and detached from the body of the carriage, and swung so low on leather braces that a person sitting inside would be no higher than standing up outside. Very convenient, indeed, for shaking hands and presenting children. The carriages and relays of horses on the road had been provided by Mr. Nathaniel Walker, the regular stage-driver on the route from Boston to Concord, N. H.

Since it was the end of June, there was an abundance of flowers blooming in New England, and it is probable that most of the countryside was stripped bare by enthusiastic well-wishers along Lafayette's route. Bouquets were thrown into the General's open barouche in such quantity that it was necessary for the driver to stop every so often in isolated spots to throw the flowers out.

In Derry Depot, New Hampshire, a young boy had been given the honor of ringing the meeting-house bell until Lafayette's carriage had passed by. When the barouche was in sight the boy found he could not ring the bell and see Lafayette at the same time, and the bell ceased ringing as Lafayette approached the meeting house. Lafayette was reported to have remarked, "That boy thinks the bell is as enthusiastic as he is, and will keep on ringing while he is looking."

An eyewitness to Lafayette's reception in Concord recalled many years later, "Many conventions have been held in Concord, it has been honored by the visits of five Presidents of the United States— Washington, Monroe, Jackson, Polk, and Grant; and it witnessed the great 'log cabin' display of 1840; but never was seen on any other occasion, such a public display and deep-toned enthusiasm as attended the reception to General Lafayette."

Lafayette went from Concord to Dover and was met at Maine's border by a deputation from that state that escorted him to Portland with a stop at Kennebunk Port. On one of Portland's triumphal arches, decorated with a small ship model, was the inscription: "I will purchase and equip a vessel at my own expense." These were the words with which Lafayette had addressed the American commissioners in Paris in 1777.

All was festive and cordial in the Portland reception and Governor Parris was a genial host to the hero. A problem arose, however, when Lafayette announced that he would leave Portland on Sunday. Governor Parris was appalled at the guest's blatant denial of the Sabbath laws and refused to accompany Lafayette out of Maine. Lafayette's only compromise was to stop long enough to attend church services at the Second Parish Unitarian Church in Biddeford, and the incident stirred up a controversy in the newspapers of Portland, Concord, and Boston.

On Sunday night Lafayette slept at Northwood and the next day stopped at Concord and traveled through Hopkinton, Brandford, and Newport to Claremont, New Hampshire. He crossed the border into Vermont on the morning of Tuesday, June 28, and proceeded to Woodstock, where he was given lunch. From there he went to Royalton for a banquet and arrived that night in Montpelier, where another banquet and reception were held. Levasseur wrote, "Although Vermont is very mountainous, which rendered the road more difficult, we travelled with extreme rapidity, advancing almost all of the time more than nine miles an hour, relays of horses having been well disposed by the inhabitants, in order that the General might not be retarded in his progress to New York." The city expected him by July 4.

The next morning Lafayette addressed the women of Montpelier and then left for Burlington, which he reached at two in the afternoon. There he was introduced to the people of the town by the governor and Lafayette received individually each of one hundred old veterans. After the public dinner Lafayette visited the university, where he had been invited to lay the cornerstone of a new building. These ceremonies over, a reception was held at the home of Governor Van Ness, at which the women of the town were introduced to Lafayette. Levasseur observed, "In the state of Vermont, as in all the rest of the Union, the females are not strangers either to the principles of government, or to the obligations of patriotism; their education, more liberal than in any part of Europe, places them in a condition more worthy the rank of thinking beings."

There were two steamboats, the *Phoenix* and the *Congress,* waiting on the shore of Lake Champlain to carry Lafayette's entourage across the lake to New York State. Amidst the farewells of the people of Burlington and a thirteen-gun salute, Lafayette boarded the *Phoenix* and members of the Vermont legislature and a large number of citizens followed in the other boat.

The next day, June 30, Lafayette disembarked at Whitehall under a canopy of two hundred flags of all nations. After welcoming ceremonies and a noonday banquet the citizens of Whitehall furnished new carriages and horses to enable him to travel as rapidly as possible to Albany, where he would board the boat to New York. He arrived in Albany at two the next afternoon, attended a performance of *Honey Moon* at the theater, and a banquet. Late that night he boarded the S.S. *Bolivar* and went as far as West Point, where he transferred to the *James Kent.* He arrived in New York City early on the morning of July 4.

A great many outsiders had come into New York for the July 4 celebration in 1825, for it had been announced that General Lafayette would be on hand to help with the celebration. At midnight, before Lafayette's arrival, a discharge of artillery announced the commencement of the forty-ninth anniversary of American independence and by morning the militia were under arms and the streets, public places, and entrances to churches were thronged with people.

One of the major events of the day was the laying of the cornerstone of the new building that would house the Mechanic's Library of Brooklyn. Some years later an eyewitness to this event, Walt Whitman, recalled his personal impressions of the ceremony:

It was in 1824 (or '25, I am not certain which, I was a little "kid" of five or six years old) I remember it was an exceptionally pleasant and sunny forenoon. At that time the reception of a public man, or other festival of the kind, was very different from anything of the sort now—was quite informal and old-fashioned, without the crowds, and blare and ceremony of the present day; but was full as hearty & far less tedious. The people on this occasion all turned out and formed on both sides of a hollow cave nearly two miles long, thickly fringed with well dress'd humanity, women as well as men, the children placed in front. That was about all, yet it was singularly effective. Lafayette came over on a Fulton Ferry (then called the Old Ferry) in a large canary-colored open barouche, drawn by four magnificent white horses, I think there was no band of music, and I think no speechifying (or if so, only a few brief words)—but a marked profusion of young children, and old men (several of the latter were revolutionary soldiers) and a number of blacks freed from slavery by the then late New York emancipation acts. These diversified the main assemblage which was composed of substantial Brooklyn citizens with their wives.

Through all, the carriage of the noble Frenchman was very slowly driven. I remember that the fine horses attracted my attention fully as much as the great visitor himself. The whole thing was curiously magnetic and quiet. He was evidently deeply pleased and affected. Smiles and tears contended on his homely yet most winning features.

But the principal incident in my recollection is now to come. They were at that time just commencing the foundation of the Brooklyn Apprentices Library, and Lafayette had consented to lay the cornerstone with his own hands—that is to grasp it personally. Some half a mile or so over from the ferry, he stopt, got out of the barouche, and in the midst of the crowd, with other gentlemen, assisted in lifting the children, amid the deep-cut excavation and heaps of stones, to safe spots where they could see the ceremony. Happening to stand near, I remember I was taken up by Lafayette in his arms and held a moment—I remember that he press'd my cheek with a kiss as he set me down—the childish wonder and nonchalance during the whole affair at the time,—contrasting with the indescribable preciousness of the reminiscence since.

I remember quite well Lafayette's looks, tall, brown, not handsome in the face, but of fine figure and the pattern of goodnature, health, manliness, and human attraction (a life size full length oil-painting exhibited years ago in Philadelphia, in 1877, I think, seems to me an admirable likeness as I recollect him at the time.)

That beautiful sunshiny day, over sixty years since, the spontaneous effusion of all stages of humanity, and the occasion, made a picture, which time has continued to set deeper and deeper in my recollection.

The portrait mentioned by Whitman had been painted by Samuel F. B. Morse during Lafayette's previous trip to New York and was later exhibited at the Philadelphia centennial celebration. It was commissioned by and is owned by the city of New York.

After the Brooklyn ceremonies a procession of tradesmen was formed to escort Lafayette back into the city and as many as could fit then attended church services and heard a reading of the Declaration of Independence. Following this a banquet and reception were held at City Hall and the major decoration was an armchair used by Washington as President that had been decorated with branches of laurels and evergreens. That evening there were gala performances at the Park Theatre and Castle Garden.

"After the exertions of such a day," wrote Levasseur, "the General required rest, and the citizens, always attentive to his wishes, allowed him, during some days, freely to enjoy the calmer and not less pleasant attentions of his private friends." However, on July 5 Lafayette did attend an exhibition of "transparent paintings" and on Friday night he went to the Chatham Theatre, where he saw Mrs. Waring perform as "Lydia Languish" in *The Rivals.* The next evening he cut a ribbon at Castle Garden, which allowed the ascension of the balloon *American Star.*

By this time plans were being made for Lafayette's trip back to France and he had decided that this time he would allow the government to provide the ship in which he would travel. Through correspondence with President Adams he became convinced that this was an offer he should not refuse and on July 13 he wrote to Thomas Jefferson, "I think, all considered, I have done well to yield to the President's proposal and to the people's wish in accepting my passage on board the frigate most kindly named the Brandywine."

22

TO PHILADELPHIA AND A
RETURN TO WASHINGTON

It was now the middle of July and Lafayette, despite entreaties from officials and friends that he send for his family and remain permanently in the United States, decided that it was time for him to return to France. The decision was made to depart before winter set in, but before he left Lafayette had a few last commitments to fulfill. He had only two months left and he set out again for Pennsylvania. On his way he would pass through New Jersey for more celebrations.

Lafayette's desire to revisit Philadelphia was spurred by his promise to attend the dedication ceremonies of the water works being constructed there, as Levasseur explained:

We had visited, during our first stay in Philadelphia, the fine machinery established on the Schuylkill, for the supplying of water to a population of one hundred and twenty thousand persons, and we had been struck with the simplicity of its mechanism, its admirable force, the elegance and good taste of the building prepared for its protection; however, then being pressed with other engagements, we but slightly glanced at its general aspect, without entering into examination of details, and it was to supply this defect of our information that we returned hither a second time with the committee entrusted with the superintendence of the expenses of the establishment.

It was excessively hot in Philadelphia during Lafayette's second visit. The thermometer rose as high as 104 degrees on some days, but this seemed not to deter Lafayette from keeping a full and taxing schedule. He attended all festivities planned for the occasion and for the last time visited his many friends in the area. He called the water works "the perfect representation of the American government, in which were combined simplicity, power and economy." Following his inspection he was given a miniature model of a vertical section of the water works, executed in mahogany.

Lafayette, George, and Auguste were guests at the State of Schuylkill, a private organization that had been founded in 1731. There they were made honorary "citizens" of the benevolent society and presented with the "national" costume, fisherman's hats.

They then were given a boat and spent the afternoon fishing in the river, catching an abundant supply of fish, which was cooked for them. Levasseur wrote, "Never was a repast attended with greater gaiety, nor cheered by better wine, and long shall we have the pleasure of remembering the delight and good cheer we found in the State of Schuylkill."

After leaving Philadelphia Lafayette boarded the steamboat *Delaware* to go to Wilmington, where many citizens had gathered to accompany him to the Brandywine battlefield. This was the first stop of many on his way to Baltimore, at which he finally arrived on the morning of July 30, and he spent two relatively quiet days there.

On August 1 Lafayette said goodbye to his friends and left for Washington, accompanied by two members of the Baltimore Committee on Arrangements. A few miles outside of Washington he was met by an elegant carriage containing President Adams' eldest son, sent by his father to invite the General and his companions to stay at the Executive Mansion. This caused some consternation on the part of Lafayette's Baltimore escorts, who had not anticipated such a breach in the prearranged plans. They argued that Lafayette was a guest of the people and as such should not stay anywhere but hotels and houses where arrangements had already

73. Photograph of painting of reception for Lafayette at Chew House in Philadelphia. *From an old print*

been made. Both men were ardent supporters of Andrew Jackson and were therefore hostile to any decision made by John Quincy Adams. Lafayette accepted the invitation and there was little for the two men to do but to express their disapproval and go alone to a Washington hotel. However, when they later received special invitations to dine with the President and Lafayette that evening they overlooked their political principles and attended.

This period in the President's house was obviously enjoyed by Levasseur, who later wrote about it:

The lodgings prepared for us in his own house by the president were plain, but commodious and in good taste. Anxious to enable General Lafayette to enjoy the repose he thought him to need after so many and such long voyages, and after numerous and profound emotions, he secluded himself with us in entire privacy. Aided by Mrs. Adams, her two sons, and two nieces, he made us taste, if I may so express myself, the sweets of domestic life. During the early portion of our stay, there rarely set down to table or around the hearth more than two or three persons at once, and usually these were some public officers who, after being occupied all day with the president in business, were detained by him to dinner and the familiar conversation of the evening.

Lafayette expressed a desire to visit James Monroe one last time and the President offered to accompany him. The party set out on the sixth of August for Oak Hill, a trip of thirty-seven miles. Adams, Lafayette, George, and another person rode in one carriage and Levasseur and the President's son followed in a smaller carriage. They took no military escort and traveled as private citizens. It was excessively hot and Monroe and his neighbors quietly entertained the illustrious guests indoors for their two-day visit. On the trip back one of Mr. Adams' horses dropped from apoplexy and the travelers were forced to wait by the side of the road while a fresh horse was brought. No passersby recognized them.

Lafayette also made a final visit to the homes of Jefferson and Madison and visited some towns along the way. James Monroe accompanied Lafayette on his journey to Monticello and Montpelier and Chief Justice Marshall also took part in some of the celebrations in the area. The General spent some final days at Monroe's home and on August 25 he returned to Washington. He was to leave the city one last time before he boarded the ship that would take him back to France.

23

LAFAYETTE'S FAREWELL
TO AMERICA

Upon entering office John Quincy Adams had decided that it would be appropriate for the American people to provide a public ship for Lafayette's return to France. A vessel was built in the Washington Navy Yard and was launched at the end of June. It would be ready for sea duty at the beginning of September, the time Lafayette had chosen for his departure. Adams wrote the following letter to the General:

It is customary to designate our frigates by the names of rivers of the United States; to conform to this custom, and make it accord with the desire we have to perpetuate a name that recalls that glorious event of our revolutionary war, in which you sealed with your blood your devotion to our principles, we have given the name of Brandywine to the new frigate, to which we confide the honourable mission of returning you to the wishes of your country and family. The command of the Brandywine will be entrusted to one of the most distinguished officers of our navy, Captain Charles Morris, who has orders to land you under the protection of our flag, in whatever European port you please to designate.

The day of sailing was set for September 7, and on Saturday, August 27, Lafayette, Captain Morris, and President Adams consulted on the detail of the departure and voyage.

From Monday to Wednesday Lafayette was in Mount Vernon for a final visit with descendants of George Washington and when he returned he again had dinner with President Adams. He spent his last days in Washington visiting with friends and writing letters of regret to the many towns and villages he had been unable to visit. On September 4 he wrote to Thomas Jefferson, "We leave here for the Brandy Wine on the 7th. My heart is too full to write more. A thousand blessings on you and your family."

One last great celebration had been planned for the night before Lafayette's departure. September 6 was the General's sixty-eighth birthday and President Adams gave a state dinner to celebrate the occasion. All public officers and the many distinguished citizens from many states who had come to see Lafayette off were invited and farewell gifts were presented to him. The New York delegation's present was an account of all the events occurring during Lafayette's visits in New York City. The volume was magnificently bound and its fifty pages were ornamented with vignettes of views and portraits. The artists were Burton, Inman, and Cummings and the writing was done by Mr. Bragg. The presentation book was made of American paper and had been bound in New York. As it was passed around and admired the President and each member of his Cabinet placed his signature in the book.

The cheer that prevailed through hundreds of banquets given that year in Lafayette's honor was missing at the President's birthday and farewell dinner. "Although a large company partook of this dinner," Levasseur recalled later, "and it was intended to celebrate Lafayette's birthday, it was very serious; I may say almost sad. We were all too much pre-occupied by the approaching journey to be joyous; we already felt, by anticipation, the sorrowfulness of separation."

The next day, Lafayette's day of departure, "dawned radiantly." A holiday had been declared in Washington and the stores remained closed and workshops deserted. Crowds gathered at the President's mansion and the militia were drawn up in a line along the route Lafayette was to take to the river. At eleven o'clock Lafayette left his apartments and slowly passed through the group of privileged people who had been able to gain access to the interior of the house. He entered a room where the President and his Cabinet, various public officers, and private citizens waited for him. He took his place in the center of this crowd and the doors of the Executive Mansion were thrown open so that those outside might observe the proceedings. John Quincy Adams then delivered his farewell address to Lafayette:

It has been the good fortune of many of my distinguished fellow-citizens, during the course of the year now elapsed, upon your arrival at their respective places of abode, to greet you with the welcome of the nation. The less pleasing task now devolves upon me, on bidding you, in the name of the nation, adieu.

It were no longer seasonable, and would be superfluous, to recapitulate the remarkable incidents of your early life—incidents which associated your name, fortunes, reputation, in imperishable connection with the independence and history of the North American Union.

The part which you performed at that important juncture was marked with characters so peculiar, that, realizing the fairest fable of antiquity, its parallel could scarcely be found in the authentic records of human history.

You deliberately and perseveringly preferred toil, danger, the endurance of every hardship, and the privation of every comfort, in defence of a holy cause, to inglorious ease, and the allurements of rank, affluence, and unrestrained youth, at the most splendid and fascinating court of Europe.

That this choice was not less wise than magnanimous, the sanction of half a century, and the gratulations of unnumbered voices, all unable to express the gratitude of the heart with which your visit to this hemisphere has been welcomed, afford ample demonstration.

When the contest of freedom, to which you had repaired as a voluntary champion, had closed, by the complete triumph of her cause in this country of your adoption, you returned to fulfill the duties of the philanthropist and patriot in the land of your nativity. There, in a consistent and undeviating career of forty years, you have maintained, through every vicissitude of alternate success and disappointment, the same glorious cause to which the first years of your active life had been devoted, the improvement of the moral and political condition of man.

Throughout that long succession of time, the people of the United States, for whom, and with whom you had fought the battles of liberty, have been living in the full possession of its fruits; one of the happiest among the family of nations. Spreading in population; enlarging in territory; acting and suffering according to the condition of their nature; and laying the foundations of the greatest, and, we humbly hope, the most beneficent power that ever regulated the concerns of many upon earth.

In that lapse of forty years, the generation of men with whom you co-operated in the conflict of arms, has nearly passed away. Of the general officers of the American army in that war, you alone survive. Of the sages who guided our councils; of the warriors who met the foe in the field or upon the wave, with the exception of a few, to whom unusual length of days has been allotted by heaven, all now sleep with their fathers. A succeeding, and even a third generation, have arisen to take their places; and their children's children, while rising up to call them blessed, have been taught by them, as well as admonished by their own constant enjoyment of freedom, to include in every benison upon their fathers, the name of him who came from afar, with them in their cause to conquer or to fall.

The universal prevalence of these sentiments was signally manifested by a resolution of congress, representing the whole of the United States to communicate to you the assurances of grateful and affectionate attachment of this government and people, and desiring that a national ship might be employed, at your convenience, for your passage to the borders of your country.

The invitation was transmitted to you by my venerable predecessor; himself bound to you by the strongest ties of personal friendship, himself one of those whom the highest honours of his country had rewarded for blood shed early in her cause, and for a long life of devotion to her welfare. By him the services of a national ship were placed at your disposal. Your delicacy preferred a more private conveyance, and a full year has elapsed since your landing upon our shores. It were scarcely an exaggeration to say, that it has been, to the people of the Union, a year of uninterrupted festivity and enjoyment, inspired by your presence. You have traversed the twenty-four states of this great confederacy: you have been received with rapture by the survivors of your earliest companions in arms: You have been hailed as a long absent parent by their children, and men and women of the present age: And a rising generation, the hope of future time, in numbers surpassing the whole population of that day when you fought at the head and by the side of their forefathers, have vied with the scanty remnants of that hour of trial, in acclamations of joy at beholding the face of him whom they feel to be the common benefactor of all. You have heard the mingled voices of the past, the present, and the future age, joining in one universal chorus of delight at your approach; and the shouts of unbidden thousands, which greeted your landing on the soil of freedom, have followed every step of your way, and still resound, like the rushing of many waters, from every corner of our land.

You are now about to return to the country of your birth, of your ancestors, of your posterity. The executive government of the Union, stimulated by the same feeling which had prompted the congress to the designation of a national ship for your accommodation in coming hither, has destined the first service of a frigate, recently launched at this metropolis, to the less welcome, but equally distinguished trust, of conveying you home. The name of the ship has added one more memorial to distant regions and to future ages, of a stream already memorable, at once in the story of your sufferings and of our independence.

The ship is now prepared for your reception, and equipped for sea. From the moment of her departure, the prayers of millions will ascend to heaven that her passage may be prosperous, and your return to the bosom of your family as propitious to your happiness, as your visit to this scene of your youthful glory has been to that of the American people.

Go, then, our beloved friend—return to the land of brilliant genius, of generous sentiment, of heroic valour; to that beautiful France, the nursing mother of the twelfth Louis, and the fourth Henry; to the native soil of Bayard and Coligni, of Turenne and Catinat, of Fenelon and D'Aguesseau. In that illustrious catalogue of names which she claims as of her children, and with honest pride holds up to the admiration of other nations, the name of Lafayette has already for centuries been enrolled. And it shall henceforth burnish into brighter fame; for if, in after days, a Frenchman shall be called to indicate the character of his nation by that one individual, during the age in which we live, the blood of lofty patriotism shall mantle in his cheek, the fire of conscious virtue shall sparkle in his eye, and he shall pronounce the name of Lafayette. Yet we, too, and our children, in life and after death, shall claim you for our own. You are ours by that more than patriotic self-devotion with which you flew to the aid of our fathers at the crisis of their fate. Ours by that long series of years in which you have cherished us in your regard. Ours by that unshaken sentiment of gratitude for your services which is a precious portion of our inheritance. Ours by that tie of love, stronger than death, which has linked your name, for the endless ages of time, with the name of Washington.

At the painful moment of parting from you we take comfort in the thought, that wherever you may be, to the last pulsation of your heart, our country will be ever present to your affections; and a cheering consolation assures us, that we are not called to sorrow most of all, that we shall see your face no more. We shall indulge the pleasing anticipation of beholding our friend again. In the meantime, speaking in the name of the whole people of the United States, and at a loss only for language to give utterance to that feeling of attachment with which the heart of the nation beats, as the heart of one man—I bid you a reluctant and affectionate farewell.

Lafayette, affected upon hearing what was, in essence, his eulogy, could not reply to the speech immediately. An approving murmur spread through the crowds inside and outside the room who had been able to hear Adams' speech. Lafayette, having heard and made so many emotional speeches in the past year, regained his composure and gave his last speech in America:

Amidst all my obligations to the general government, and particularly to you, sir, its respected chief magistrate, I have most thankfully to acknowledge the opportunity given me, at this solemn and painful moment, to present the people of the United States with a parting tribute of profound, inexpressible gratitude.

To have been, in the infant and critical days of these states, adopted by them as a favourite son, to have participated in the toils and perils of our unspotted struggle for independence, freedom and equal rights, and in the foundation of the American era of a new social order, which has already pervaded this, and must, for the dignity and happiness of mankind, successively pervade every part of the other hemisphere, to have received at every stage of the revolution, and during forty years after that period, from the people of the United States, and their representatives at home and abroad, continual marks of their confidence and kindness, has been the pride, the encouragement, the support of a long and eventful life.

But how could I find the words to acknowledge that series of welcomes, those unbounded and universal displays of public affection, which have marked each step, each hour, of a twelve-months' progress through the twenty-four states, and which, while they overwhelm my heart with grateful delight, have most satisfactorily evinced the concurrence of the people in the kind testimonies and the immense favours bestowed on me by the several branches of their representatives, in every part and at the central seat of the confederacy?

Yet, gratifications still higher await me; in the wonders of creation and improvement that have met my enchanted eye, in the unparalleled and self-felt happiness of the people, in their rapid prosperity and insured security, public and private, in a practice of good order, the appendage of true freedom, and a national good sense, the final arbiter of all difficulties, I have had proudly to recognise a result of the republican principles for which we have fought, and a glorious demonstration to the most timid and prejudiced minds, of the superiority, over degrading aristocracy or despotism, of popular institutions founded on the plain rights of man, and where the local rights of every section are preserved under a constitutional bond of union. The cherishing of that union between the states, as it has been the farewell entreaty of our great paternal Washington, and will ever have the dying prayer of every American patriot, so it has become the sacred pledge of the emancipation of the world, an object in which I am happy to observe that the American people, while they give the animating example of successful free institutions, in return for an evil entailed upon them by Europe, and of which a liberal and enlightened sense is everywhere more and more generally felt, show themselves every day more anxiously interested.

And now, sir, how can I do justice to my deep and lively feelings for the assurances, most peculiarly valued, of your esteem and friendship, for your so very kind references to old times, to my beloved associates, to the vicissitudes of my life, for your affecting picture of the blessings poured by the several generations of the American people on the remaining days of a delighted veteran, for your affectionate remarks on this sad hour of separation, on the country of my birth, full, I can say, of American sympathies, on the hope so necessary to me of seeing again the country that has designed, nearly half a century ago, to call me hers? I shall content myself, refraining from superfluous repetitions, at once, before you, sir, and this respected circle, to proclaim my cordial confirmation of every one of the sentiments which I have had daily opportunities publicly to utter, from the time when your venerable predecessor, my old brother in arms and friend, transmitted to me the honourable invitation of congress, to this day, when you, my dear sir, whose friendly connection with me dates from your earliest youth, are going to consign me to the protection, across the Atlantic, of the heroic national flag, on board that splendid ship, the name of which has been not the least flattering and kind among the numberless favours conferred upon me.

God bless you, sir, and all who surround us. God bless the American people, each of their states, and the federal government. Accept this patriotic farewell of an overflowing heart; such will be its last throb when it ceases to beat.

At his closing words Lafayette threw himself into the arms of the President as both cried "Adieu! Adieu!" The spectators wept along with Adams and Lafayette and the General retired to his apartments to collect himself. There he was visited by Mrs. Adams, her daughters, and her nieces, who came to express their good wishes and regrets. As a parting gift, the previous evening, the First Lady had presented to Lafayette a bust of her husband and a book of French verses she had written herself.

The first of twenty-four guns signaled to Lafayette that it was time to leave and he embraced John Adams once more before he walked down the steps of the White House. The President waved goodbye from the top step and this was also a signal for the colors of the troops that were drawn up before the President's house to be bowed to the ground.

With an escort of the Secretaries of State, Treasury, and the Navy, Lafayette proceeded to the banks of the Potomac, where the steamboat *Mount Vernon* waited for him. All the militia of Alexandria, Georgetown, and Washington were standing in columns on the bank of the river. The crowds were led by the officials of three cities and when Lafayette arrived at the point of embarkation the descendants of George Washington and the principal officers of the government drew around him for a final farewell as the troops filed past. Accompanying him on the *Mount Vernon* were the Secretary of the Navy and other officers of government who had been specially chosen for this honor. A "mournful cry" was heard above the sounds of the artillery as Lafayette boarded the boat. This was an expression of farewell from the crowds. The guns were fired from Fort Washington and a repetition of the cry was emitted from the people lined up on the shores of all the towns the boat passed.

General Lafayette was received on board the *Brandywine,* anchored at the mouth of the Potomac, with greatest honors. The yards were manned, the gunners were at their posts, and the Marines were drawn up on deck. The only official to accompany Lafayette on board the *Brandywine* was Mr. Southard, Secretary of the Navy. He presented Lafayette and recommended him to the care of Commodore Morris in the name of the American nation and its government and then left the ship.

Just as Morris was about to give the command to weigh anchor a steamship was seen approaching the *Brandywine*. It contained a huge deputation from Baltimore, who insisted on saying a final "adieu" to Lafayette. They boarded the frigate and by the time they left it was too late to set sail and Commodore Morris waited until the next day, September 8, to start the voyage. It was not until the ship had passed through Chesapeake Bay and into ocean waters that Captain Morris was free to present himself to Lafayette and to announce to the General that the last orders he had received before sailing were that he was to place himself and the *Brandywine* at the General's disposal and to conduct him to any port he should desire. Lafayette asked for passage to Havre, but the ceremony was only a courtesy, for the arrangements already had been discussed at length in Washington and the Lafayette family had been told of the approximate date and place of embarkation and were making plans to meet the General at the port.

On the voyage, two days out, there was a violent storm that caused the illustrious passengers and many of the crew to succumb to seasickness. The new frigate leaked badly and the pumps could not keep up with the water that poured into her. Captain Morris wisely ascertained that the ship was too deep in the water and ordered thirty-two thousand pounds of iron ballast thrown overboard. This solved the problem and made it an easier matter to discover the sources of leaks, which were just under the water line and were repaired. The remainder of the voyage was comfortable.

The *Brandywine* had an interesting crew. When it was being made up so many midshipmen petitioned the President to join the ship on its historic maiden voyage that Adams decided that each

74. Allegorical print of Lafayette on deck of the *Brandywine*. Gods are driving away unfavorable winds and Washington and Franklin are with Lafayette in spirit. Print was originally at La Grange. *Photograph courtesy of State Street Bank and Trust Company, Boston*

76. Scene from base of *Brandywine* presentation vase, "Brandywine arriving at Havre." *Photograph courtesy of State Street Bank and Trust Company, Boston*

77. Detail from vase "The Capitol at Washington." *Photograph courtesy of State Street Bank and Trust Company, Boston*

75. Silver gilt and enameled vase presented by midshipmen of the *Brandywine* to Lafayette shortly after his return to France. *Photograph courtesy of State Street Bank and Trust Company, Boston*

78. Detail from vase "Lafayette at Washington's Tomb." Other two figures may represent George Washington Lafayette and Auguste Levasseur. *Photograph courtesy of State Street Bank and Trust Company, Boston*

of the twenty-four states in the Union should be represented. A ship the size of the *Brandywine* would ordinarily require ten midshipmen, but the decision to use the larger group was made as a compliment to Lafayette. As a tribute to the General, the crew, at the termination of the voyage, commissioned the American consul in Paris, Mr. Barnett, to have a silver presentation urn made and this was sent to La Grange as a souvenir of the trip shortly after Lafayette's return to his estate.

The ocean voyage took twenty-four days and while waiting near the port of Havre for a pilot boat to lead the frigate into port Lafayette received letters advising him that his family and many friends were waiting at Havre to receive him. Some of the citizens of the town came on board during this time and before Lafayette left the frigate the officers surrounded him for a final farewell. The first lieutenant, Mr. Gregory, had been chosen by the crew to make the speech, but he was so overcome with emotion that his voice faltered when he started to talk. Instead he ran to the stern of the ship and grabbed the American flag that flew there. As he presented it to Lafayette he exclaimed, "We cannot confide it to more glorious keeping! Take it, dear General, may it forever recall to you your alliance with the American nation; may it also sometimes recall to your recollection those who will never forget the happiness they enjoyed of passing twenty-four days with you on board of the *Brandywine;* and in being displayed twice a year on the towers of your hospitable dwelling, may it recall to your neighbors the anniversary of two great epochs, whose influence on the whole world is incalculable,—the birth of Washington and the declaration of the independence of our country."

The inspired gesture greatly touched Lafayette, who answered, "I accept it with gratitude, and I hope that, displayed from the most prominent part of my house at La Grange, it will always testify to all who may see it, the kindness of the American nation towards its adopted and devoted son. And I also hope, that when you or your fellow countrymen visit me, it will tell you that at La Grange you are not on foreign soil."

Cannons and the cheers of sailors in the navy yards of Havre welcomed Lafayette to his own country as he disembarked with Captain Morris, who had been assigned to accompany Lafayette into Paris. The *Brandywine,* under the command of Lieutenant Gregory, sailed for duty in the Mediterranean.

The people of the United States were to honor General Lafayette one last time after his famous tour. When news of his death reached these shores in 1834, John Quincy Adams, now a member of Congress, moved a resolution "to consider and report by what token of respect and affection it may be proper for the Congress of the United States to express the deep sensibility of the Nation to the event of the desease of General LAFAYETTE." A committee was appointed in the house consisting of one member from each state. Adams was appointed chairman. The Senate then passed a resolution on June 21 and a joint committee was formed. On June 24 the joint committee made its report:

Resolved by the Senate and House of Representatives of the United States of America in Congress assembled, That the two Houses of Congress have received, with the profoundest sensibility, intelligence of the death of General LAFAYETTE, the friend of the United States, the friend of WASHINGTON, and the friend of liberty.

And be it further resolved, That the sacrifices and efforts of this illustrious person in the cause of our country, during her struggle for Independence, and the affectionate interest which he has at all times manifested for the success of her political institutions, claim from the Government and People of the United States an expression of condolence for his loss, veneration for his virtues, and gratitude for his services.

And be it further resolved, That the President of the United States be requested to address, together with a copy of the above resolutions, a letter to GEORGE WASHINGTON LAFAYETTE, and the other members of his family, assuring them of the condolence of this whole Nation in their irreparable bereavement.

And be it further resolved, That the members of the two houses of Congress will wear a badge of mourning for thirty days; and that it be recommended to the People of the United States to wear a similar badge for the same period.

ORATION

ON THE

LIFE AND CHARACTER

OF

GILBERT MOTIER DE LAFAYETTE.

DELIVERED

AT THE REQUEST OF BOTH HOUSES OF THE

CONGRESS OF THE UNITED STATES,

BEFORE THEM,

IN THE HOUSE OF REPRESENTATIVES

AT WASHINGTON,

On the 31st of December, 1834.

By JOHN QUINCY ADAMS,

A MEMBER OF THE HOUSE.

WASHINGTON:
PRINTED BY GALES AND SEATON.
1835.

81. *Above.* Cover of booklet published by Congress and containing oration given in Congress at news of death of Lafayette. *Benjamin DeForest Curtiss Collection, Watertown Library*

79. *Top left.* Lafayette medal, designed to honor the hero during his visit to America in 1824 and 1825, was struck again after his death. *De Witt Collection, University of Hartford*

80. *Below left.* Reverse of medal worn after Lafayette's death. Inscribed "Lafayette/born Sepr 6, 1757/died May 20, 1834/in the 77 year of his age/the hero of two hemispheres/the generous noble minded/liberal philanthropist/the brave and chivalrous/soldier and single/hearted patriot." *De Witt Collection, University of Hartford*

And be it further resolved, That the Halls of the House be dressed in mourning for the residue of the session.

And be it further resolved, That John Quincy Adams be requested to deliver an Oration on the Life and Character of General LAFAYETTE, before the two Houses of Congress, at the next session.

The resolution was passed unanimously and printers all over the country went to work to supply mourning badges to the thousands who could boast that they had once seen, touched, marched with, or been kissed by, the great Lafayette.

John Quincy Adams, happier in his congressional role than he had been as President, gave his memorial oration on December 31, 1834, before both Houses and on request presented a copy of the address for publication. On January 6, 1835, it was moved that "——— copies of the oration be printed for the use of the House" to communicate "through the medium of the press" to give the public access to the speech. The Chair said that it was necessary to fill in the blank, to decide exactly how many copies should be printed, and after some deliberation it was decided that fifty thousand copies should be made available to the House of Representatives. On motion of Henry Clay ten thousand more copies were printed for the Senate. In this manner a nation that had paid tribute to the hero during his lifetime showed its affection for him after his death.

BIBLIOGRAPHY

BARBAROUX, CHARLES OGE, AND LARDIER, JOSEPH. *Voyage du Général Lafayette aux Etats Unis d'Amerique en 1824.* Paris: L'Huillier, 1824.

BIOGRAPHICAL NOTICE OF GENERAL LAFAYETTE: *Translated from Notice Biographique sur le Général Lafayette and Accompanied with a Portrait and the Original Work in French.* Philadelphia: B. Tanner, 1824.

BIOGRAPHICAL SKETCH OF GENERAL DE LAFAYETTE WITH THE EXCEPTION OF THOMAS SUMPTER, THE ONLY SURVIVING MAJOR-GENERAL OF THE AMERICAN REVOLUTION. Philadelphia: printed for T. Wilson by J. Bioren, 1824.

BRANDON, EDGAR EWING. *A Pilgrimage of Liberty: A Contemporary Account of the Triumphal Tour of General Lafayette Through the Southern and Western States in 1825, As Reported by the Local Newspapers.* Athens, Ohio: The Lawhead Press, 1944.

BRANDON, EDGAR EWING. *Lafayette, Guest of the Nation.* Oxford, Ohio: Oxford Historical Press, 1950.

BUTLER, FREDERICK. *Memoirs of the Marquis de La Fayette, Major-general in the Revolutionary Army of the United States of America: Together with His Tour of the United States.* Wethersfield, Connecticut.: Deming and Francis, 1825.

CANFIELD, MAY GRACE. *Lafayette in Vermont.* Privately printed, 1934.

CHINARD, GILBERT. *When Lafayette Came to America.* Easton, Pennsylvania: American Friends of Lafayette, 1948.

DANGERFIELD, GEORGE. *The Era of Good Feelings.* New York: Harcourt, Brace & World, Inc., 1952.

DAVIS, EDWARD H. *The Lafayette Presentation Button, 1824.* Waterbury, Connecticut: The Mattatuck Historical Society, Occasional Publications New Series No. 18, April 1951.

DE LA BEDOYERE, MICHAEL. *Lafayette, a Military Gentleman.* New York: Charles Scribner's Sons, 1934.

DUBERGIER (TRANSLATOR). *Histoire du Général de Lafayette, par un citoyen Americain; Traduite de l'Anglais par M. B.* Paris: Chez Ponthieu, Libraire, Palais Royal, 1825.

ELLIOT, SAMUEL. *An Humble Tribute to My Country, or, Practical Essays,*

Political, Legal, Moral, and Miscellaneous, Including a Brief Account of the Life, Sufferings and Memorable Visit of General Lafayette. Boston: Otis, Broaders and Company, 1842.

FARMER, LYDIA HOYT. *The Life of La Fayette, the Knight of Liberty in Two Worlds and Two Centuries.* New York: T. Y. Crowell & Company, 1888.

FISHBACK, FREDERICK LEWIS. *"The Congressional Reception of Lafayette One Hundred Years Ago," Columbia Historical Society Records,* Washington, D.C., 1924.

FORBES, ALLAN, AND CADMAN, PAUL F. *France and New England.* Boston: State Street Trust Company of Boston, 1925.

FOSTER, JOHN. *Sketch of Tour of Lafayette.* Portland, Maine: Printed at Statesman office by A. W. Thayer, no date.

GOTTSCHALK, LOUIS REICHTENTHAL. *Lafayette Comes to America.* Chicago: University of Chicago Press, 1935.

HISTORICAL SKETCHES ILLUSTRATIVE OF THE LIFE OF M. DE LAFAYETTE; *And the Leading Events of the American Revolution.* New York: 1824.

HONOUR TO THE BRAVE: *A Description of the Grand Fete Given at Washington Hall, by the Citizens of France to Gen. Lafayette.* New York: 1824.

HUME, EDGAR ERSKINE. *La Fayette and the Society of the Cincinnati.* Baltimore: The Johns Hopkins Press, 1934.

HUME, EDGAR ERSKINE. *Lafayette in Kentucky.* Frankfort, Kentucky: Transylvania College and the Society of the Cincinnati in the State of Virginia, 1937.

HUNGERFORD, ARTHUR E. (COMPILER). *Lafayette and Baltimore.* Baltimore: The Saint James Publishing Company, 1924.

HUNT, W. G. *An Oration in Honor of Gen. Lafayette Delivered in His Presence in Nashville, May 4, 1825.*

JENKINS, CHARLES FRANCIS. *Lafayette's Visit to Germantown, July, 1825: An Address Delivered Before the Pennsylvania Geneological Society, March, 1909.* Philadelphia: W. J. Campbell, 1911.

KLAMKIN, MARIAN. *American Patriotic and Political China.* Charles Scribner's Sons: New York, 1973.

KLAMKIN, MARIAN. *The Collector's Book of Bottles.* New York: Dodd, Mead and Company, 1971.

KNAPP, SAMUEL LORENZO. *Memoirs of General Lafayette, with an Account of His Visit to America, and of His Reception by the People of the United States; From His Arrival, August 15th, to the Celebration at Yorktown, October 19th, 1824.* Boston: E. G. House, 1824.

LA FAYETTE. Hartford, Connecticut: Barber and Robinson, 1825.

LAFAYETTE. *Lafayette to the People.* Originally published in the *Kentucky Gazette,* 1825.

LAFAYETTE AT BRANDYWINE. West Chester, Pennsylvania: Chester County Historical Society, no date.

LATZKO, ADREAS. *Lafayette: A Life.* New York: The Literary Guild, 1936.

LEVASSEUR, AUGUSTE. *Lafayette in America in 1824 and 1825; or Journal of a Voyage to the United States.* Translated by John D. Godman, M. D. Philadelphia: Carey and Lea, 1829.

LOVELAND, ANNE C. *Emblem of Liberty: The Image of Lafayette in the American Mind.*

LOWRY, R. *Lafayette, a Complete History, Etc., by an Officer in the Late Army, New York.* Hartford: S. Andrews and Company, 1850.

MAUROIS, ANDRES. *Adrienne: The Life of the Marquise de La Fayette.* New York: McGraw Hill, 1961.

MCKEARIN, HELEN. *Bottles, Flasks and Dr. Dyott.* New York: Crown Publishers, Inc., 1970.

MEMOIRS OF THE MILITARY CAREER OF THE MARQUIS DE LA FAYETTE, DURING THE REVOLUTIONARY WAR, DOWN TO THE PRESENT TIME, INCLUDING HIS RECEPTION IN NEW YORK, BOSTON, AND THE PRINCIPAL TOWNS IN NEW ENGLAND, CAREFULLY COMPILED FROM THE MOST AUTHENTIC SOURCES. Boston: Allen and Watts, 1824.

NEW YORK (CITY). *The Pamphlet, Containing a Description of the Grateful Manner in Which the Whole Population of the City of N. Y. Received Gen. Lafayette on the 16th of August, 1824, and the Very Affectionate Manner They Expressed Their Farewell on the Memorable 14th July, 1825; Together with a Description of the National Festival, Given by the Honourable the Corporation of the City of New York, in Commemoration of the Glorious Fourth of July, 1776.* New York: 1825.

NOLAN, JAMES BENNET. *Lafayette in America Day by Day.* Baltimore: The Johns Hopkins Press, 1934.

PARKER, AMOS ANDREW. *Recollections of General Lafayette on His Visit to The United States, in 1824 and 1825, with the Most Remarkable Incidents in His Life, from His Birth to the Day of His Death.* Keene, New Hampshire: Sentinel Printing Company, 1879.

PEMBER, JAY READ. *A Day with Lafayette in Vermont.* Woodstock, Vermont: The Elm Press, 1912.

PICTORIAL LIFE OF GENERAL LAFAYETTE: *Embracing Anecdotes Illustrative of His Character.* Philadelphia: Lindsay and Blakiston, 1847.

ROBERTS, OCTAVIA. *With Lafayette in America, with Illustrations from Old Prints.* Boston and New York: Houghton Mifflin Company, 1919.

SEDGWICK, HENRY DWIGHT. *Lafayette.* Chautauqua, New York: The Chautauqua Press, 1928.

SWEENEY, JOHN A. H. *Lafayette in the Decorative Arts.* New York: *Antiques,* pp. 136–40, August 1957.

TOTH, DAVID GOLDSMITH. *The People's General; The Personal Story of Lafayette.* New York: Charles Scribner's Sons, 1951.

WHITMAN, WALT. *Lafayette in Brooklyn; With an Introduction by John Burroughs.* New York: G. D. Smith, 1905.

WILLIAMS, W. T. *An Account of the Reception of General Lafayette in Savannah.* Savannah, Georgia: 1825.

INDEX